Hilary Walden is a well-known
seventeen books, and a regular c
Taste and *House and Garden*.

By the same author

—

SERVES ONE

HILARY WALDEN

GRAFTON BOOKS

A Division of the Collins Publishing Group

LONDON GLASGOW
TORONTO SYDNEY AUCKLAND

Grafton Books
A Division of the Collins Publishing Group
8 Grafton Street, London W1X 3LA

A Grafton Paperback Original 1991
9 8 7 6 5 4 3 2 1

A CIP catalogue record for this book
is available from the British Library

ISBN 0-586-20926-3

Printed and bound in Great Britain by
Collins, Glasgow

Set in Meridien

Contents

INTRODUCTION

The number of people who, like me, cook only for one is much larger than is often realized, and larger even than the number of one-person households suggests. The statistics do not take into account those who share accommodation with others yet cook for themselves, or married people whose 'other half' is away for a short while. Yet the vast majority of cookery books, recipes in magazines and even manufacturers' promotional recipes make four or more servings.

There are people who will make do with snacks or convenience foods, rather than cooking just for themselves, but current thinking is moving away from ready-prepared foods to fresh ones. While some people are happy with plain grills, the proportion of people catering for one who want imaginative, up-to-date recipes at least some of the time is as high as in the rest of the population, and it is for these that this book is intended.

Virtually all the recipes make enough for one serving only, which avoids the all-too common problem of having to eat the same dish twice, the reincarnated version a pale imitation of its original self. The few exceptions to this can all be given a different guise the second time around, and will be just as good as on their first appearance.

I have avoided recipes that require a lot of ingredients because the list itself can be offputting and often seems out of proportion when it is just for one person. Also, the amount of each item needed for one person may be so small that some ingredients, such as vegetables, may be only partially used, while others become difficult to measure. I have also tended to avoid dishes with subtle, intricate blends of flavourings as it is not really practical to make dishes for one which require a lot of spices, herbs or other flavourings.

Shopping and cooking for one is now much easier than it used to be. Not only do supermarkets sell fruit and vegetables loose, but a growing number of greengrocers, even in small towns and some villages, have adopted the self-service system. This makes it possible to avoid the situation that many people dread of having to ask for a couple of carrots, two onions and an apple, to the disapproval of the shop assistant who has to weigh them out. Supermarkets also sell individual cuts of meat and fish, which saves possible embarrassment at the butcher's and fishmonger's.

Cooking just for one definitely has its advantages. There is less shopping to carry, and preparing a single portion takes less time because there is less chopping etc., while some tasks, such as removing mussels from their shells and peeling fresh prawns, that sometimes seem too laborious to attempt when catering for larger numbers, do not take any time at all. The cooking time is usually shorter – small pans do not take as long to heat up as large ones, liquids come to the boil more quickly, and when boiling vegetables, for example, it takes far less time for water to return to the boil after the vegetables have been added.

Moreover, you can afford to fiddle around and adjust flavours etc. to get the dish the way *you* like it.

I have included some recipes that could be classed as snacks but there is a little more to them than just opening a packet, and they show that a snack need not be all stodge and fat, or devoid of any nutritional value at all.

Although some recipes use, for example, only half an avocado, they are cross-referenced to other recipes that you could make to use the remaining half. It is a good idea to think about this in advance so you can make sure you have the necessary ingredients in store.

Equipment

Very little equipment is vital for making the recipes in this book. Whereas a selection of good knives definitely makes life much easier when cooking for a number of people, when preparing food for one you can get by with just one good-quality, all-purpose knife with a serrated blade. The one I use most has an 11cm/4½in blade.

As far as pans, bowls, cooking dishes and electrical equipment are concerned, think small. There are plenty of small sizes available, which have the advantages of being cheaper than the larger versions and taking up less room in the cupboard. The pan I use most is a 13.5cm/5½in nonstick saucepan, followed by a 17.5cm/7in frying pan and a small butter-warmer for making simple sauces. When you are using only small amounts it can be very difficult to prevent food cooking too quickly in pans (it is especially difficult to keep liquids simmering gently), and great care is needed to stop them burning. To overcome this problem I use a metal heat-diffusing mat. Good-quality heavy pans, always a sound investment, make even more sense when cooking small quantities as they help to prevent food cooking too quickly and 'catching'. Although top-quality pans are more expensive, the cost of the smaller ones is not as prohibitive as that of family-sized pans. Nonstick surfaces are a valuable asset. My favourite casserole is a heavy, enamelled 15cm/6in cast-iron one. A couple of different-sized ramekin dishes come in handy, as do two flameproof gratin dishes, one round, one oval, about 13.5–15cm/5½–6in round or long. However, if you do not have the appropriate-sized dish you can sometimes improvise by moulding a double thickness of foil into the necessary shape and placing it in a larger dish. To steam foods I use a colander over a saucepan of boiling water for small quantities and a steaming basket for larger ones.

Very few of the recipes in this book need to be cooked in the oven because it may not seem worth heating it up for small quantities. Instead, I have devised ways of making greater use of the grill and steamer to cook, among other things, super-light soufflés, and food wrapped in foil or in a foil-covered heatproof dish.

I always used an oven thermometer to test the recipes in this book that were cooked in the oven, but as all ovens vary and oven thermostats are notoriously inaccurate, do keep an eye on how things are cooking.

A small blender is well worth having as it makes light work of so many tasks.

Ingredients

Unsalted butter and olive oil   Although these may seem expensive they work out cheaper than you might think, because only small amounts are needed at a time. Their superior flavour is instantly noticeable whenever they are used. Keep the oil in a cool, dark place, but not the fridge.

Herbs   It is becoming far easier to obtain fresh herbs all the year round as so many supermarkets and good greengrocers have some available all the time. In the summer it is very simple for almost everyone to grow a few varieties themselves, such as parsley, chives and mint. A garden is not necessary; tubs on a patio, a window box, or indoor pots on a windowsill will do.

Summer-grown herbs have the best flavour, and as the flavour of most frozen herbs is much better than dried ones I often freeze some. Commercially frozen herbs are also available.

Spices   I invariably use whole spices as I find buying ground ones very wasteful; their flavour deteriorates so quickly that most of it has vanished before it is used and the remaining spice has to be thrown away.

To prevent unnecessary flavour loss from spices, keep them in a cool, dark cupboard.

My store cupboard and fridge provide me with much of the

inspiration I need when cooking. Listed below are some items I find very useful for quickly and easily adding the variety and special touches to food that help prevent monotony creeping in, which in turn can lead to not bothering to cook at all. Most can now be bought from good supermarkets, as well as specialist food shops. Store-cupboard ingredients for desserts are listed on page 210.

A vast range is not necessary. It is far better to have just a few well-chosen, good-quality, versatile ingredients that you enjoy, and will use quite often, rather than a vast number that are used infrequently.

Sauces Horseradish, pesto, Tabasco, Worcestershire, anchovy paste or purée (more convenient than cans of anchovy fillets), garlic purée, tapenade and anchoïaide, tahina, soy sauce.

Oils Mild olive oil for cooking, a fruity one for salad dressings, walnut and hazelnut oils for dressings, sesame oil for stir-frying and dressings.

Vinegars Good-quality white and red wine vinegars, tarragon vinegar, genuine Spanish sherry vinegar and Italian balsamic vinegar.

Beans and pulses Ready prepared in cans for salads, sauces and soups. Lentils do not need to be soaked so can be bought in packets.

Preserves Olives (vacuum-packed large black Greek ones, green Spanish 'queens' packed in brine, green and black ones steeped, separately, in oil and herbs), capers, sun-dried tomatoes bottled in olive oil, fruits bottled in alcohol for instant indulgent puddings with crème fraîche, fromage frais or Greek yogurt.

Dry goods Couscous, which only needs to be heated through (it is not very difficult to buy the traditional type that has to be cooked), and bulgur, which does not need cooking. The only recipes that require flour are Crumbles (see page 233) and Sweetcorn Drop Scones (see page 86).

Fresh root ginger Root ginger freezes well and the amount needed for a specific dish can be grated off the still frozen piece, which can then be put back in the freezer.

Dried mushrooms These are very useful both for boosting the flavour of white cultivated mushrooms and as a substitute for wild ones. Dried ceps and morels can be bought from good grocers, delicatessens and supermarkets, Chinese black mushrooms from Chinese food shops.

Dried mushrooms may at first sight seem an extravagance but their flavour is so good that only small amounts are needed. Before using them, soak them in a little hot water for 20–30 minutes, drain off the water, but do not throw it away – strain it and either use in the same dish or keep it for another one.

Sun-dried tomatoes preserved in oil These have a concentrated, rich flavour and are needed only in small amounts. Slice them and toss with pasta or rice, use with stir-fry dishes, or to boost the flavour of dishes using fresh tomatoes when they are insipid.

Quantities

Where the quantity of an ingredient is given as approximate it is because appetites and tastes vary, and within the basic framework there is often leeway for individuals to make adjustments to suit their own needs and preferences.

Similarly, there is often scope for flexibility in the choice of ingredients, as you will notice in the number of alternatives and variations that I have given.

SOUPS

Making your own soup need not take hours. Interesting, well-flavoured soups, tasting much better than anything from a packet or can, can be quick and easy to prepare, whether for a first course or a main course.

Soups offer plenty of scope for improvisation, depending on what ingredients you have available; they can be thickened with potato, oats ground to flour in a blender, ground nuts, creamed coconut, or an egg. An egg also makes it more nourishing, but do make sure you heat the soup slowly, stirring constantly, after adding the egg, and do not allow the mixture to boil. Stir in cream, Greek yogurt, fromage blanc or soft cheese for a creamier taste and texture.

Below is an all-purpose recipe that can be used as the foundation of a wide range of vegetable soups, adding flavourings (mustard, pesto, ginger, orange and lemon juices and rinds, spices, herbs etc.) as appropriate and adjusting the consistency and creaminess, if necessary, after the cooking.

1 spring onion or 1 small shallot, chopped
unsalted butter
approximately 115–150g/ 4–5oz vegetables (prepared weight)
200–225ml/7–8fl oz chicken or vegetable stock, or water

2 tablespoons double cream, Greek yogurt or fromage blanc
salt and freshly ground black pepper
good bread or savoury toasts (see pages 29–43), to serve

Cook the spring onion or shallot in a little melted butter until softened but not coloured. Stir in the vegetables, cover and leave to cook gently over a low heat for about 5 minutes, shaking the pan occasionally. Add the stock, bring to the boil then cover the pan and leave to simmer gently for 15–20 minutes or until the vegetables are tender.

Purée the soup, return to the pan and heat through thoroughly. Add the cream, yogurt or fromage blanc and heat through again. Adjust the seasoning.

VARIATIONS

- Replace some or all of the stock with milk.
- Fry bacon with the spring onion or shallot, or add some diced cooked gammon or ham with the stock, water or milk.
- Substitute a small leek for the spring onion or shallot.
- Add a small chopped stick of celery.
- Use combinations of vegetables – examples which work well together include potato with watercress or leeks, parsnip and watercress, broccoli and cauliflower, mushrooms with spinach or watercress.
- Garnish the soup with herbs, diced or crumbled cooked bacon, or plain or flavoured croutons (see page 62).
- Artichoke and Sage – add a couple of fresh sage leaves, or a very small pinch of dried sage, with the stock.
- Broad Bean and Hazelnut – add about 1 tablespoon chopped, toasted hazelnuts when heating the soup after puréeing.

- Broccoli and Brie or Camembert – stir 40–55g/1½–2oz diced Brie or Camembert, with the rinds removed, into the soup when heating after puréeing.
- Broccoli and Lemon – add about ½ teaspoon finely grated lemon rind and 1 teaspoon lemon juice with the broccoli; adjust if necessary with the final seasoning.
- Carrot and Coriander – add 1–1½ teaspoons crushed coriander seeds with the spring onion or shallot.
- Carrot and Orange – add a little grated orange rind and orange juice about 5 minutes before the soup is ready. Orange also goes well with parsnip.
- Cauliflower and Cardamom – add the crushed seeds from 3 cardamom pods with the spring onion or shallot. Cardamom also goes well with carrot.
- Cauliflower Cheese – use half stock and half milk. Stir about 2 teaspoons finely grated mature Cheddar cheese into the soup after puréeing and take care not to let the soup boil when reheating. Sprinkle about 20g/¾oz grated cheese over to serve.
- Celery and Stilton – use half stock and half milk and add about 40g/1½oz crumbled Stilton when puréeing the soup. Add a little lemon juice and flavour with a very small pinch of freshly grated nutmeg.
- Fennel and Almond – use half stock and half milk. Stir 1 tablespoon ground almonds into the lightly cooked vegetables, and serve garnished with lightly toasted flaked almonds.
- Lettuce and Almond – use 85–115g/3–4oz lettuce and reduce the stock to 115ml/4fl oz (this applies whenever making lettuce soup). Add 1 tablespoon ground almonds with the stock and serve the soup garnished with lightly toasted flaked almonds.
- Mushroom and Nutmeg – flavour the soup with a little freshly grated nutmeg before puréeing. Nutmeg is also a good flavouring for cauliflower and spinach.
- Curried Parsnip – add about 1 teaspoon curry powder with the spring onion or shallot.

- Parsnip and Ginger – add about ½ teaspoon grated fresh root ginger just before adding the parsnips.
- Potato and Chive – add chopped chives about 5 minutes before the soup is ready.

——————— *Lentil and Cumin Soup* ———————

This is a meal in itself when accompanied by a crisp salad and good bread.

Whole green or brown lentils have more flavour than split red ones, but these could be substituted, if wished. Different vegetables could also be used – for example, substitute 1 leek for the celery and omit the shallot.

1 shallot, chopped
1 small clove garlic, crushed
olive oil or unsalted butter
pinch cumin seeds
30g/1oz whole green or brown lentils
1 small bay leaf and 2 parsley sprigs, tied together if liked

1 small carrot, chopped
1 small stick celery, chopped
1 tomato, skinned and chopped
salt and freshly ground black pepper
chopped fresh parsley, to serve

Gently cook the shallot and garlic in a little oil or butter with the cumin seeds, stirring occasionally, for 3–4 minutes. Add the lentils, stir for a couple of minutes then add 300ml/½ pint water and the herbs. Bring to the boil then reduce the heat and simmer gently for 40 minutes.

Meanwhile, cook the carrot, celery and tomato in a little butter or oil in a covered pan over a low heat for about 15 minutes, shaking the pan occasionally.

When the lentils are cooked add the vegetables with their

cooking juices and simmer gently for a further 15 minutes. Remove the herbs, and season to taste. Purée the soup, if liked. Serve sprinkled with chopped parsley.

—————— *Corn Chowder* ——————

1 rasher bacon (I prefer to use smoked), chopped
unsalted butter
1 spring onion or 1 small shallot, finely chopped
1 small potato, diced
½ bay leaf
pinch chopped thyme, or very small pinch dried thyme
85g/3oz sweetcorn – fresh,
thawed frozen, or drained canned
115ml/4fl oz milk
2 tablespoons single cream (optional)
chopped fresh parsley or chives
lemon juice
salt and freshly ground white or black pepper

Cook the bacon in a little butter, stirring occasionally, until the bacon is crisp and the fat has run. Remove about a third, using a slotted spoon, and reserve. Stir the chopped spring onion or shallot into the pan and cook over a low heat, stirring occasionally, until softened but not coloured. Stir in the potato then 85ml/3fl oz water and the herbs. Bring to the boil, cover and simmer gently for about 15–20 minutes or until the potatoes are almost tender. Stir in the sweetcorn and simmer again, this time uncovered, for 5 minutes. Add the cream, if using, and a little parsley or chives, and heat through but do not boil. Add a little lemon juice and season with pepper and just a little salt. Serve with the remaining bacon sprinkled over.

VARIATION
• Add about 85g/3oz lightly poached smoked haddock cut into chunks, or about 55g/2oz diced smoked chicken, or the same

quantity of smoked oysters or mussels, or prawns with the sweetcorn and keep the liquid so that it barely simmers.

Haricot Bean and Basil-flavoured Soup

This recipe, using a whole can of haricot beans, serves two good-sized portions, but can easily be halved if you want to use half the beans in another recipe – try substituting them for flageolet beans in Tuna and Flageolet Bean Salad (see page 57).

unsalted butter
1 onion, finely chopped
600ml/1 pint vegetable stock
425g/15oz can haricot beans, drained and rinsed

2–3 tablespoons pesto
salt and freshly ground black pepper
chopped fresh parsley and tomato, for garnish

Heat a little butter, add the onion and cook until softened but not coloured. Add about 425ml/¾ pint of the stock, bring to the boil then cover and simmer for about 15 minutes. Purée, return to the pan, and add the beans and pesto, then simmer for 5 minutes, stirring occasionally. Taste and adjust the seasoning and the amount of pesto, if necessary.

Serve sprinkled with chopped parsley and tomato.

Coconut and Cardamom Soup

A good homemade chicken stock (see page 245) is essential for this soup.

seeds from 2 green cardamom pods, lightly crushed
1 spring onion or small shallot, finely chopped
1 tablespoon dry white port or vermouth
150ml/5fl oz chicken stock, preferably jellied
15g/½oz creamed coconut (from a block)
2–3 tablespoons single cream
salt and freshly ground white pepper

Heat the cardamom seeds in a heavy, preferably nonstick pan over a medium heat for about 3 minutes to bring out the flavour. Add the onion or shallot and port or vermouth, reduce the heat, then cover and cook until the onion has softened but not coloured, shaking the pan occasionally. Increase the heat and boil until the port or vermouth has almost completely evaporated. Stir in the stock and bring to the boil. Reduce the heat and simmer gently for about 5 minutes.

Meanwhile, chop the coconut in a blender. Pour in the soup and cream and blend until smooth. Adjust the seasoning and reheat gently – do not allow to boil.

BREAD-BASED MEALS

Both the quality and variety of breads have improved so much recently that bread can provide the foundation, and inspiration, of many meals. The uses of bread go far beyond a slice of toast for breakfast, or a sandwich, although of course sandwiches and 'things on toast' can make quite substantial and nourishing snacks. If served on a plate with a salad and eaten with a knife and fork rather than 'on the run', they can also make quite a respectable light meal or supper. There are myriad ingredients and combinations of ingredients that can be served on toast and most people have their own preferences, or improvise with what is available, so I have given only a few of my own particular favourites. Instead I have concentrated on ways of making bread into interesting homemade snacks – so much healthier than shop-bought crisps etc. – or accompaniments to almost any dish, either as well as potatoes, rice or pasta, or instead of them.

Bread is very adaptable and has many other uses – for example, as a substitute for pastry in tartlet cases or to cover casseroles. Arrange slightly overlapping slices, circles or strips of bread over the top of a casserole, brush them with melted butter and bake for 15–20 minutes until crisp and golden. This is a good way of making a second helping out of a dish that has its own sauce, or can be moistened by the addition of a sauce. So is spooning a filling into bread cases, or covering it with a savoury gratin topping made by sprinkling a mixture of breadcrumbs, grated cheese, and some chopped herbs, if liked, over the top, dribbling over melted butter, or dotting with diced butter then baking at 200°C/400°F/gas mark 6 until the top is golden.

Bread Cases

Far easier, and lighter, than pastry cases, these can be made to whatever size you want, and you can either make just enough for one meal or prepare several and keep the remainder in an airtight container in a cool place for about six days.

If you cook the cases beneath the grill, keep an eye on them to make sure they brown evenly and do not burn.

Either cut the crusts from slices of bread or, for a neater shape, use a plain biscuit cutter or a thin glass to cut the bread into circles. Brush the bread well on both sides with oil or melted unsalted butter and fit into tart, muffin or Yorkshire pudding tins. Bake at 180°C/350°F/gas mark 4 for about 15 minutes, or place on the lowest rung beneath a moderately low grill until golden.

Breadcrumb Cases

For 4 7.5cm/3in cases, put 55g/2oz fresh breadcrumbs, 40g/1½oz ground almonds, 55g/2oz chopped nuts, 1 crushed clove garlic and ½ teaspoon dried mixed herbs in a blender or food processor and process finely. Add 1½ tablespoons melted unsalted butter and seasoning to taste then press into the tartlet tins. Bake at 180°C/350°F/gas mark 4 for about 20–25 minutes or until crisp.

Bread Roll Cases

These can be used instead of vol-au-vent cases. Either cut bread rolls in half or cut a slice off the top, depending on the size of the roll and the size of case you want. Scoop out the crumbs from the roll, leaving a wall about 1.25cm/½in thick; take care not to pierce the outer shell. Brush well inside and out with melted butter or oil, not forgetting the lid if a slice has been cut off. Place on a baking sheet and bake at 180°C/350°F/gas mark 4 for 5–10 minutes or until crisp.

For extra flavour, use a garlic or other-flavoured oil, or sprinkle paprika pepper or finely grated cheese over the inside of the shell.

Bread cases can be made from individual brioches – simply break off the topknot and proceed as above.

Bread recipes for sweet snacks and desserts are on page 226–33.

Avocado on Rye

2 lean rashers streaky bacon, chopped
1 small avocado
1 slice from a large rye or brown caraway seed loaf
dash tarragon vinegar
watercress, for garnish

Cook the bacon in a small, nonstick pan until crisp. Meanwhile, mash half the avocado then season. Slice the other half.

Toast the bread on both sides then spread immediately with the mashed avocado. Arrange the sliced avocado on top. Add a dash of vinegar to the bacon then spoon it on to the avocado slices. Garnish with watercress and eat immediately.

——————— *Smoked Salmon Bagels* ———————

This is not too expensive if smoked salmon trimmings are used.

2 bagels
70g/2½oz low- or full-fat soft
    cheese
1 tablespoon chopped fresh
    dill
1 teaspoon lemon juice

salt and freshly ground black
    pepper
approximately 40g/1½oz
    smoked salmon, cut into
    strips
dill sprigs, for garnish

Quickly warm the bagels in the oven or under the grill. Meanwhile beat together the cheese, dill, lemon juice and seasonings – go easy with the salt because of the salt in the salmon.

Split open the bagels and cut the tops in half. Spread the bases with the cheese mixture, place strips of smoked salmon on top. Put on the tops and garnish with sprigs of dill.

VARIATIONS
- Use other rolls instead of bagels.
- Substitute prawns or smoked trout for the smoked salmon.
- Substitute chives or basil for the dill.

——————— *Chicken, Mushroom and* ——————— *Watercress Sandwich*

This recipe looks deceptively long but it really takes very little time to prepare as it is a succession of quick stages, each one following on from the other. It is substantial enough for a lunch or supper dish.

salt and freshly ground black pepper

115g/4oz chicken breast, cut in half lengthways

unsalted butter and olive oil

1 spring onion, finely chopped

55g/2oz oyster, shiitake or brown (chestnut) mushrooms

2 slices bread, or a long roll or length of baguette cut in half

1 teaspoon tarragon vinegar

2 teaspoons chicken stock, white wine or dry vermouth, or use water

small sprig fresh tarragon, or small pinch dried tarragon

approximately 30g/1oz watercress, large stalks and stems removed

1–1½ tablespoons mayonnaise

watercress sprigs, for garnish

Season the chicken lightly then fry briefly in a little hot butter and oil until lightly browned on the outside and just cooked through. Transfer to absorbent paper and keep warm. Add the spring onion then the mushrooms to the pan and cook over a moderate heat, stirring occasionally, for a couple of minutes. Using a slotted spoon, remove the mushroom and onion and keep warm. Start to toast the bread or roll, and meanwhile stir the vinegar and the stock, wine, vermouth or water into the pan. Add the tarragon, stir briefly then stir in the watercress, coating the leaves with the liquid. Remove, using a slotted spoon. Remove the pan from the heat.

Cut the chicken into strips. Stir the mayonnaise into the pan then spread it over the hot toast, cover with the mushroom and watercress mixture then place the chicken strips on top. Garnish with watercress sprigs.

VARIATION

- Fry some toasted sesame or sunflower seeds with the mushrooms, and sprinkle a few more over the chicken before serving.

——— *Mushroom and Anchovy Sandwich* ———

2 slices fresh Granary or
   medium rye bread
1–2 tablespoons soured cream,
   chilled
sliced raw mushrooms

1 anchovy fillet, soaked for 10
   minutes, drained and
   chopped
lemon juice
approximately 1 teaspoon
   finely chopped fresh dill

Spread the bread generously with the soured cream. Cover one slice with the mushrooms, scatter the pieces of anchovy over then sprinkle with lemon juice and the chopped dill. Top with the remaining slice of bread and eat immediately.

VARIATION
- Lay some watercress leaves on the soured cream before adding the mushrooms.

——— *'Pizza' Roll* ———

40g/1½oz sliced salami,
   roughly chopped
1 large ripe tomato, skinned,
   seeded and chopped
3 stoned green olives, sliced
30g/1oz Mozzarella or Bel
   Paese cheese, grated

freshly ground black pepper
10cm/4in length French
   bread, or 1 long crisp roll
unsalted butter, for spreading
chopped fresh chives

Mix the chopped salami, tomato, olives and half the cheese together. Season with black pepper.

   Cut the bread or roll in half lengthways and toast on both sides then butter generously, sprinkle with chopped chives and cover with the salami mixture. Top with the remaining cheese and place under a hot grill until the cheese has melted.

VARIATIONS
- Brush the toast with olive oil instead of spreading with butter.
- Rub the toast with garlic.
- Substitute toasted crumpets, muffins, or 1 or 2 slices of Granary bread as a base.

—————————— *Pan Bagnat* ——————————

This is really a glorified (and glorious) large, moist salad sandwich from the south of France. The bread is usually from a baguette but a crisp roll could be used instead.

approximately 15–20cm/ 6–8in length baguette
good fruity olive oil
wine vinegar (optional)
salt and freshly ground black pepper
1 clove garlic, crushed
some thinly sliced Spanish onion, or spring onions

½ small red pepper, cut into thin strips
1 large, or 2 small tomatoes, thinly sliced
anchovy fillets, soaked and drained
black olives, stoned and quartered
chopped fresh basil or parsley

Split the baguette lengthways. Make a simple dressing of oil, vinegar and seasoning and sprinkle it over the cut surfaces of the bread; alternatively just sprinkle with oil and seasoning. Rub the bread with the garlic. Lay the sliced onion, pepper and tomato on top of one piece, arrange the anchovy fillets and olives on top, sprinkle with basil or parsley and cover with the other piece of bread. Press together firmly then wrap tightly in foil, place a weight on top and leave in a cool place for at least a couple of hours. Serve cut into slices.

Asparagus Rolls

Make these for a snack or savoury, or cut them into slices and serve with mayonnaise and a small salad for a light lunch. Take as part of a packed meal or to have mid-morning, or mid-afternoon. Well-drained canned or thawed frozen asparagus could be used, but it tends to be softer than fresh and you may need three spears per slice of bread.

Per roll:
2, or 3 if very slim, green asparagus spears, or 1 fat white one, trimmed
1 thin slice bread from a square-shaped loaf –

Granary and wholegrain are good
salt and freshly ground black pepper
melted unsalted butter
freshly grated Parmesan

Steam the asparagus for about 10 minutes so it remains crisp. Refresh in cold running water, drain and leave to dry on absorbent paper.

Place each slice of bread in turn between 2 sheets of grease-proof paper and roll out thinly, using a rolling pin. Remove the bread from the paper, brush one side of each slice with melted butter. Lay an asparagus spear diagonally across one corner of each slice, sprinkle with a little black pepper then roll up the asparagus in the bread.

Brush the outside with melted butter then roll in freshly grated Parmesan cheese to coat evenly.

Place the rolls, seam-side down, on a baking sheet and place under a moderate grill until crisp and golden. Eat hot.

VARIATIONS
- Coat the rolls in sesame seeds instead of Parmesan.
- Lay a thin slice of smoked salmon, smoked trout or Parma ham on the bread before adding the asparagus. Coat in sesame seeds.

- Spread the bread with a little mild mustard.
- Spread the bread lightly with soft cheese or mayonnaise instead of butter.

Fried Cheese Roll-ups

These can be served as a snack, a savoury first course, or an accompaniment to a vegetable soup.

2 slices bread, crusts removed
approximately 30g/1oz hard
   cheese, such as mature
   Cheddar, Gruyère,
   Emmenthal or goat's cheese,
   cut into 2.5cm/½in
   matchsticks

1 small egg
milk
approximately ½ teaspoon
   Worcestershire sauce
oil or butter, for frying

Roll out each slice of bread separately between 2 sheets of greaseproof paper. Place a cheese matchstick at one edge of each slice and roll up, Swiss-roll fashion.

Beat the egg with a drop of milk and the Worcestershire sauce. Dip the rolls in the egg mixture to coat evenly then remove, allowing the excess to drain off. Fry in hot butter or oil until crisp and golden and serve hot.

VARIATIONS
- Omit the Worcestershire sauce, and spread the bread with pesto.
- Cover the bread with a thin slice of ham.

Sesame Roll-ups

These crunchy, moist, nutty rolls are delicious eaten with soup or salads, or just on their own. If you do not have a rolling pin, use a bottle to roll out the bread.

2 slices bread, preferably
    wholemeal, crusts removed
approximately 40g/1½oz full-
    fat soft cheese

approximately 15g/½oz
    sesame seeds

Place each slice of bread in turn between 2 sheets of greaseproof paper and roll out thinly with a rolling pin. Remove the bread from the paper, cut each slice in half then spread both sides of each piece with the soft cheese.

Place some of the sesame seeds on one of the pieces of greaseproof paper then roll up each piece of bread lengthways, Swiss roll-fashion, coating it in the sesame seeds. Add more seeds to the greaseproof paper as they are used up.

Place the rolls under the grill, turning them, until they are evenly browned. Serve hot.

VARIATION
- Spread the bread with anchovy purée or paste instead of or as well as soft cheese.

Savoury Toasts

The following recipes use bread for snacks, impromptu first courses, as accompaniments to drinks, soups or salads, or even for eating with main courses.

Sesame Toasts

A very simple way to make bread a little different, and one of my favourites for using the tail end of yesterday's baguette.

French baguette, fairly thinly   unsalted butter
  sliced   sesame seeds

Toast the baguette slices on one side then lightly spread the untoasted side with butter. Sprinkle sesame seeds over and grill until golden brown. Serve warm.

Anchovy Toasts

The simplest of savouries that are very 'moreish' to eat for a snack, with drinks:

Anchoïaide (see page 241)   tomato slices
French bread slices

Spread anchoïaide on slices of French bread, then bake in a hot oven until crisp. Top each one with a slice of tomato.

Herb Toasts

unsalted butter, softened   French bread slices
garlic purée   chopped fresh herbs
freshly ground black pepper

Flavour the butter with garlic purée and black pepper. Spread generously on the bread then place under a moderate grill until the edges of the bread are slightly browned. Sprinkle with the herbs.

VARIATIONS
- Sprinkle with grated Parmesan or Gruyère cheese after grilling.
- Top toasted bread with a slice of tomato then sprinkle with the herbs.
- Sprinkle with capers, chopped black olives, or chopped sun-dried tomatoes then sprinkle with herbs.
- Sprinkle the plain version, or cheese variation, with chopped, grilled, smoked bacon.

Bruschetta

In Latium and Abruzzi, thick slices of bread are grilled over charcoal then rubbed with crushed garlic and finished with a dribble of good olive oil. In the absence of a charcoal grill, either bake the bread (outside Italy, French bread is usually used) at 180°C/350°F/gas mark 4 for 10–15 minutes until crisp, or toast under a moderate grill. While still hot rub the top with cut garlic, pour a little green olive oil over and sprinkle with salt and freshly ground black pepper.

VARIATIONS
- Top with a slice of tomato and a basil leaf.
- Spread with anchoïaide, tapenade or pesto.
- Spread with beaten Ricotta cheese and sprinkle with chopped black olives.
- Spread with Tarragon and Mustard Mayonnaise (see page 238).

Spring Onion Toasts

approximately 2 tablespoons
   mayonnaise – a tarragon-
   flavoured one is good
approximately 2–3 teaspoons
   finely grated Parmesan
   cheese

approximately ½ teaspoon
   Dijon mustard, to taste
2 slices baguette, cut on the
   diagonal
chopped spring onion

Mix the mayonnaise, Parmesan and mustard together, adjusting the proportions, to taste. Toast the baguette slices on both sides, spread one side of each slice with the mayonnaise and place under the grill until lightly warmed. Sprinkle with chopped spring onion.

Mustard Pitta Fingers

Serve with vegetable soups, egg dishes, chicken or beef.

small wholemeal pitta breads
butter

wholegrain or herb mustard

Open the pitta bread out to form a pocket. Butter the inside then spread with mustard. Close the pitta bread and press lightly together. Toast on both sides until just beginning to change colour, cut into fingers and serve immediately.

Pesto and Tomato Baguette

2 ripe tomatoes, sliced
1 teaspoon white wine vinegar
1 tablespoon fruity olive oil
1 small clove garlic, crushed

salt and freshly ground black
   pepper
approximately 15cm/6in
   length of baguette
pesto

Lay the tomatoes in a dish. Mix the vinegar, oil, garlic and seasoning together, pour over the tomatoes, cover and leave for several hours in a cool place – the longer you leave it, the cooler the place should be.

Split the baguette and spread the cut surfaces with pesto. Place under a preheated grill for 1 minute then top each piece of baguette with tomatoes and the marinating juices and grill for a couple of minutes or so until the tomatoes are warmed through or, if you prefer, until they just colour slightly.

VARIATION
- Top the tomatoes with grated Mozzarella cheese before grilling.

Crunchy Mushroom Toasts

This may seem quite large for one serving, but mushrooms are not very substantial. However, if you want only a light snack, reduce the quantities by a third.

olive oil
small knob unsalted butter
30g/1oz cashew nuts, chopped
225g/8oz flat or cup brown
    cap (chestnut) mushrooms,
    broken into large pieces
2½ tablespoons chopped fresh
    coriander

lemon juice
salt and freshly ground black
    pepper
2 slices wholemeal or Granary
    bread
coriander sprigs, for garnish

Heat a little oil and butter, add the chopped nuts and cook until lightly browned. Stir in the mushrooms and cook over a high heat for just a few minutes, stirring frequently, until they are browned but still retain their 'bite'. Quickly stir in the coriander and add lemon juice and seasoning to taste.

Meanwhile, toast the bread and put on to a warmed plate.

Spoon the mushroom mixture and cooking juices on to the toast and garnish with sprigs of coriander.

VARIATIONS
- Use other nuts, or some sunflower seeds, instead of the cashew nuts.
- Parsley can be substituted for the coriander, although it does not give the same distinctive flavour.
- Add 1 tablespoon sherry or Madeira to the mushrooms and allow the juices to bubble so the excess moisture evaporates.

_____ *Avocado, Prawn and Horseradish* _____
Toasted Rolls

Two rolls make quite a substantial snack, but it is a useful recipe to bear in mind when you have half an avocado, as the recipe can easily be halved to make just one roll for a lighter snack.

2 tablespoons mayonnaise
approximately 2 teaspoons
   creamed horseradish, to
   taste
2 long wholemeal rolls
1 ripe avocado
55g/2oz shelled prawns

approximately ¼ teaspoon
   lemon juice
salt and freshly ground black
   pepper
slices of lemon and parsley
   sprigs, to serve

In a small saucepan, gently heat the mayonnaise and horseradish. Cut the rolls almost in half lengthways so they are hinged along one side when opened out. Lightly toast the insides.

Halve, stone and peel the avocado and slice thinly crosswise. Cover one side of each roll with overlapping slices of avocado then place under the grill for 2 minutes.

Stir the prawns into the mayonnaise and horseradish mixture, add lemon juice and seasoning to taste then spoon down the centre of each roll and top with twisted lemon slices and sprigs of parsley.

——— Mixed Vegetable Stir-fry on Toast ———

This is a good and surprisingly tasty way of taking care of odds and ends of vegetables, as it works well with many combinations. Do try always to include the sun-dried tomatoes – it's not the same at all without them.

2 teaspoons sesame oil
1 clove garlic, finely chopped
4–6 pecan halves or cashew
   nuts, roughly chopped
2 large pieces of sun-dried
   tomatoes packed in oil,
   drained and cut into thin
   strips
1 small carrot, cut into fine
   strips

white part 1 medium-sized
   leek, cut into strips
2 or 3 mushrooms, sliced
freshly ground black pepper
2 slices bread
unsalted butter
finely chopped fresh parsley
   (optional)

Heat half of the oil in a heavy nonstick, pan over a moderate heat, add the garlic and nuts and cook, stirring occasionally, for a minute or so. Stir in the vegetables and cook, stirring frequently, for 8–10 minutes. Add a spoonful of water if necessary to prevent the vegetables from sticking. Add black pepper, cover the pan and cook for a further 4–5 minutes.

Meanwhile, toast and butter the bread.

Remove the pan from the heat, stir in the parsley, if used, and the remaining sesame oil. Pile on to the hot toast.

VARIATION
● Instead of serving on toast, use the vegetables to fill an omelette.

—————— Devilled Herring Roes on Toast ——————

55g/2oz soft herring roes
unsalted butter
1 slice medium rye, Granary
   or wholemeal bread
approximately ½ teaspoon
   Dijon mustard

Worcestershire sauce
salt and freshly ground black
   pepper
parsley or coriander sprig, for
   garnish
lemon wedge

Place the herring roes in a sieve, rinse under cold running water and pat dry. Heat a little butter in a small pan, add the herring roes, cover and cook over a fairly low heat for 5–8 minutes. Meanwhile, toast the bread.

Add the mustard, a dash of Worcestershire sauce, and salt and pepper to the roes. Stir well but take care not to break up the roes, heat for a minute or so then spoon the roes and juices on to the toast. Garnish with a sprig of parsley or fresh coriander and serve with a lemon wedge to squeeze over the roes.

———— *Souffléed Cheese on Fried Bread* ————

1 egg, separated
15g/½oz Gruyère, finely
  grated
salt and freshly ground black
  pepper

1 slice French bread, or a circle
  cut from 1 slice bread such
  as Granary, wholemeal, rye
  and wholegrain, or rye and
  caraway
unsalted butter and olive oil,
  for cooking

Blend the egg yolk with the cheese and seasoning then spread on the bread.

Whisk the egg white with a very small pinch of salt until stiff. Pile on to the bread and sprinkle a little pepper over.

Using a fish slice or large spatula, transfer the bread, covered side uppermost, into hot oil and butter and cook until the bread is golden and the egg white on top lightly set.

VARIATIONS
- For a crisp top, place under a hot grill.
- Spread the toast with mustard, anchovy paste or purée, Anchoïaide (see page 241), Tapenade (see page 240), pesto, or Black Olive and Walnut Paste (see page 242) mixed with a little fromage blanc or Greek yogurt.

- A little extra cheese can be sprinkled over the top and the toast browned under a hot grill.

Cheese on Toast

Cheese on toast is more of a concept than a recipe, and can be made with an enormous variety of cheeses and breads, and different combinations of the two. They all have their own special tastes and textures; for example, Munster on Caraway Rye is completely different from Brie on Wholegrain Bread, or Stilton on Brioche, or Stilton on Wholegrain, Brie on Caraway Rye and Munster on Brioche.

People seem to have their own particular quirks for 'straight' cheese on toast – I know I have, and I'm always discovering more, so below are some recipes that have developed from the basic theme.

—————— *Cheese and Nut Soufflé Toast* ——————

1 small egg, separated
approximately 30g/1oz well-
    flavoured cheese
1 tablespoon chopped nuts –
    almonds, hazelnuts, walnuts
    or peanuts

a little parsley (optional)
double cream, Greek yogurt or
    mayonnaise
dash Worcestershire sauce
1 slice bread

Beat the egg yolk then mix in the cheese, nuts and parsley, if using. Add just enough cream, Greek yogurt or mayonnaise to moisten – barely 1 teaspoon – and add a small dash of Worcestershire sauce.

Toast both sides of the bread. Whisk the egg white until stiff then lightly fold into the cheese mixture until just evenly blended. With the hot toast still on the grill rack, cover one side with the cheese mixture. Place under the grill until puffed and golden. Eat immediately.

——————— Roquefort and Walnut Toast ———————

This can be eaten as a snack, served with drinks, or cut into squares and accompanied by a raw spinach or watercress salad.

For 1 good-sized slice of bread, mash about 25g/scant 1oz of Roquefort cheese with a very small nut of unsalted butter, a little lemon juice (or brandy) and freshly ground black pepper then mix in a heaped tablespoon of quite finely chopped walnuts.

Toast the bread then immediately spread with the cheese mixture and eat at once.

——————— Brie and Anchovy Toast ———————

approximately 55g/2oz ripe
  Brie, rinds removed
little double cream, crème
  fraîche or fromage blanc
  (optional)
freshly ground black pepper

1 slice wholegrain or Granary
  bread
½ anchovy fillet, soaked in
  milk or water, then cut into
  strips
olive oil, for brushing

Mash the Brie, adding a little cream, crème fraîche or fromage blanc, if liked, and season with black pepper.

Toast both sides of the bread then turn off the grill. Spread one side of the toast thickly with the cheese mixture. Lay the strips of anchovy on the cheese then place briefly a few inches beneath the grill to warm the top until it just begins to melt. Give it a slight spread then eat immediately.

Goat's Cheese on Toast

Goat's cheese does not melt in quite the same way as most cheeses when cooked, but goes puffy and soft, and quickly browns when it is done to the right degree. A little Parmesan cheese, olive oil or a nut oil can be sprinkled on the top for a different finish, too.

1. WITH LEEK AND WALNUTS
Serve as a first course or snack.

walnut oil
30g/1oz walnuts, roughly
   chopped
1 medium-sized leek, cut
   diagonally into
   approximately 2.5cm/1in
   slices
salt and freshly ground black
   pepper
approximately 2.5cm/1in slice
   from a wide baguette (not a
long, thin one, which will
   probably be too slim), or a
   circle cut from a thick slice
   of bread – light rye,
   wholemeal and Granary are
   all good
1 small clove garlic, peeled
   and halved
approximately 55g/2oz goat's
   cheese, preferably log-
   shaped

Heat a little walnut oil in a frying pan, add the walnuts and cook until lightly browned. Add the leek and cook over a fairly low heat for about 5 minutes, stirring occasionally. Add the seasoning.

Meanwhile, rub the bread with the garlic clove then brush with a little walnut oil. Toast on both sides until crisp and golden, place the goat's cheese on top and grill until puffy and brown.

Transfer the toast to a plate and place the leek and walnut mixture beside it.

2. WITH HERBS

Serve as a snack, either on its own or accompanied by a crisp salad. If you do not have any sun-dried tomatoes, use strips of fresh tomato, preferably skinned.

olive oil

2 slices baguette cut on a long diagonal, about 0.5cm/¼in thick

approximately 40g/1½oz soft goat's cheese

approximately 1–2 teaspoons crème fraîche, double cream or fromage blanc

approximately 1 teaspoon chopped fresh herbs, such as thyme or basil, or a very little finely chopped rosemary

1 sun-dried tomato packed in oil, drained and cut into fine strips

freshly ground black pepper

Brush a little oil on one side of the baguette slices then toast both sides lightly under a medium grill, so it becomes crisp throughout.

Mash the cheese with sufficient crème fraîche or double cream to make it spreadable. Flavour with the chopped fresh herbs, reserving a few for garnish.

Spread the cheese on the oiled side of the toast, arrange the strips of tomato on top and grind black pepper over. Place under a moderate grill until the cheese has warmed through then sprinkle the remaining herbs over.

Creamed Stilton and Almond Toasts

Good as a snack, or a first course. Add a watercress side salad for a more substantial first course or a light lunch or supper if preceded by soup or followed by a reasonably filling pudding.

2 tablespoons double cream, fromage blanc or Greek yogurt

approximately 40g/1½oz Stilton, without rind, crumbled

approximately ½ tablespoon chopped almonds

freshly ground black pepper

2 slices wholemeal French stick, cut on the diagonal

flaked almonds

Beat the cream, fromage blanc or yogurt until smooth then blend into the Stilton. Add the chopped almonds and black pepper to taste.

Toast the bread on one side. Spread the cheese mixture on the untoasted side then place under the grill until beginning to brown. Sprinkle flaked almonds over and grill until golden.

Herb Cream Cheese, Cucumber and Chive Toasts

2 slices wholegrain bread

soft cheese flavoured with herbs

chopped chives

thinly sliced cucumber

salt and freshly ground black pepper

Toast the bread on both sides then spread thickly with herb-flavoured soft cheese. Sprinkle chopped chives over the cheese then cover with slightly overlapping slices of cucumber. Sprinkle with salt and pepper and eat immediately.

VARIATION
- Substitute tomato for the cucumber.

Gorgonzola with Cucumber and Watercress on Brioche

I first made Gorgonzola, cucumber and watercress brioche to use up leftovers. The combination proved to be so successful that I often make sure I have all the ingredients together so that I can recreate it. It is by no means a definitive recipe and equally good variations can be made – the cucumber can be omitted, or replaced by chopped fresh or sun-dried tomato, for example, or the watercress can be replaced by chives (or basil, if using tomatoes). If you do not have any soft cheese, use slightly more Gorgonzola. Stilton can be used instead of Gorgonzola, and cholla, wholegrain, Granary or rye bread instead of brioche.

approximately 40g/1½oz Gorgonzola cheese, without rind
approximately 30g/1oz soft cheese
freshly ground black pepper
2 largish slices brioche
few cucumber slices
watercress leaves

Mash the cheeses together and season with black pepper. Toast the brioche slices on both sides then thickly spread one slice with the cheese. Lay the cucumber slices on top and scatter watercress leaves over. Cover with the second slice, press lightly together and serve.

Fried Sandwiches

These are notes and observations about making good fried sandwiches, rather than specific recipes for them – most people have their favourite fillings.

Do not use bread that is too fragile. Trim off the crusts, and use some oil, especially olive, for frying the sandwich, which will make it crisper and prevent too much fat being absorbed by the bread.

The most straightforward, and also the lightest, fried sandwiches can be made by sandwiching the filling, such as a slice of cheese (traditionally this is one that is firm, slices easily and melts well to give a delicious, gooey contrast to the crispness of the bread, such as Mozzarella or Gruyère, but you can use other types for different results), between two slices of bread and frying in hot oil, butter, or butter and oil, until crisp and brown. If the fat is not hot enough, the sandwich will be unappetizingly soggy and greasy. Drain the cooked sandwich on absorbent paper to soak away excess surface fat, then tuck in immediately.

More substantial fried sandwiches can be made by dipping the sandwich in beaten egg, or egg beaten with a little milk, before frying. Dipping the edges in sesame seeds or chopped nuts adds crunch as well as flavour.

As well as traditional cheeses, I also like to use softer cheeses, especially if I am dipping the sandwich in egg and milk, but the cheese must be chilled and the edges of the sandwich pressed firmly together to prevent the cheese oozing out; the edges can then be dipped in breadcrumbs, if liked, for an extra-sure seal.

Extra flavours can be introduced by spreading the bread with, for example, mustard, anchovy paste, Anchoïaide (see page 241), Tapenade (see page 240) or pesto, or topping the cheese with anchovy fillets or diced sun-dried tomatoes, or adding a slice of ham.

A piquant tomato sauce goes well with plain fried cheese sandwiches, or an anchovy one made by pounding soaked and rinsed anchovy fillets with a little olive oil to make a coarse purée then gently warming it through with a little white wine vinegar or lemon juice, and black pepper to taste; pour the warm sauce over the cooked sandwich.

VARIATION
- Smoked Haddock and Cheese Fried Sandwich – mix a little cooked and flaked smoked haddock with soft cheese and a

small amount of grated Cheddar. Season with black pepper, make a sandwich, dip in egg beaten with a little milk and fry until crisp.

Pitta Packet

1 small slice of back bacon, preferably smoked, chopped
1 shallot, finely chopped
1 wholemeal pitta bread
100g/3½oz quark or other soft cheese, flavoured with herbs or garlic, if liked
1 small egg, separated
salt and freshly ground black pepper

Fry the bacon in a nonstick pan, until the fat runs. Using a slotted spoon, transfer to kitchen paper. Add the shallot to the fat in the pan and cook, stirring occasionally, until softened. Transfer to a bowl, with the bacon.

Using a sharp knife, cut a slit along one edge of the bread to form a pocket. Place on a baking sheet.

Mix the cheese, egg yolk and seasoning with the bacon and shallot. Whisk the egg white until stiff but not dry then gently fold into the quark mixture. Spoon into the pitta packet, fold over the top then bake at 180°C/350°F/gas mark 5 for about 20 minutes or until the filling is just set. Eat straight away.

VARIATIONS
- Flavour the quark mixture with Worcestershire sauce, mustard, pesto, or finely chopped herbs.
- Fry a crushed small garlic clove with the shallot.
- Replace the bacon with ham or salami. As these do not need to be cooked, soften the shallot in a little oil.

Curried Chicken Salad Pitta

2–3 tablespoons yogurt
approximately ½ teaspoon
  curry paste, to taste
85g/3oz cooked chicken,
  chopped
5 seedless grapes, halved

6 walnut pieces
6 cucumber slices, halved
1 pitta bread
crisp lettuce leaves, shredded
watercress sprig, for garnish
  (optional)

Blend the yogurt into the curry paste, then stir in the chicken, grapes, walnuts and cucumber. With a sharp knife, slit the pitta bread along one long side then fill with shredded lettuce and the chicken mixture. Garnish with a sprig of watercress, if liked.

Mexican Turkey Pitta

olive oil
1 shallot, finely chopped
1 small courgette, chopped
1 small clove garlic, finely
  crushed
small pinch cumin seeds,
  crushed
2 ripe tomatoes
dash chilli pepper sauce
approximately 115g/4oz

cooked turkey, cut into bite-
  sized pieces
1 tablespoon chopped fresh
  coriander
salt and freshly ground black
  pepper
pitta bread
shredded crisp lettuce and
  soured cream or yogurt, to
  serve

Heat a little olive oil, add the chopped shallot and cook, stirring occasionally, until softened but not coloured. Stir in the courgette, garlic and cumin and cook, stirring, for a couple of minutes. Skin, deseed and chop the tomatoes then add, with their juices, to the pan with a very light sprinkling of chilli. Stir all the ingredients around then leave to cook, uncovered, until reduced to a thickish, slightly nubbly sauce. Stir in the turkey, allow to heat through, then add the coriander and season to taste.

With a sharp knife, slit the pitta bread along one long side then open it out to form a pocket. Put some shredded lettuce in the pitta, add the turkey mixture and top with a spoonful of soured cream or yogurt.

———— Savoury Crumble Topping ————

I find crumble toppings very useful as they are a quick and easy way of making a change from grilled and sautéed food. They also make the second day's serving of a casserole-type dish, or one that can be moistened by the addition of a sauce, that little bit different, and 'stretch' it if there isn't quite enough left for a full portion. I've also used a crumble topping to make one portion serve two when someone else has joined me for a meal at short notice.

Crumble mixtures are very simple to make, and you can use a variety of ingredients to change the flavour and texture of the basic mixture. They can be kept in an airtight container in the refrigerator, or in the freezer for up to 3 months, so are a handy standby.

The basic proportions are half as much fat as flour, with 115g/4oz flour and 55g/2oz fat usually given as the amount to serve two. I like to use a mixture of flour and breadcrumbs.

55g/2oz breadcrumbs
55g/2oz flour – white or wholemeal, or a mixture of the two, or, for a change, white with Granary or perhaps a little rye
55g/2oz unsalted butter, diced

Mix together the breadcrumbs and flour then rub in 40g/1½oz of the butter. Cover the filling with this mixture and dot the remaining butter over the surface. Bake at 180°C/350°F/gas mark 4 for 30–40 minutes until top is golden.

VARIATIONS

- Fresh breadcrumbs give an extra-light texture. Varying the type will add variety and interest. Replace a third to a half of the flour with breadcrumbs.
- For more crunch, substitute rolled oats for half the flour, or sprinkle some rolled oats over the top of the crumble.
- Add about 30g/1oz crushed savoury biscuits to the crumble mixture.
- About 55g/2oz chopped nuts added to the basic crumble will add crunch and flavour. Or sprinkle some chopped nuts over the top of a prepared crumble – don't forget peanuts, especially dry roasted ones. If they have been salted omit salt from the crumble mixture.
- Groundnuts give a closer texture and add their own flavour.
- Grated cheese melts into the other ingredients when mixed with the crumble, or some can be sprinkled over the top. Stir approximately 40g/1½oz full-flavoured cheese into the basic crumble and reduce the fat slightly.
- Chopped herbs and garlic make the crumble more savoury and can be used to emphasize or complement the filling. Stir about 2 teaspoons chopped fresh herbs into a crumble mixture based on 115g/4oz flour.
- Give the top extra crispness and crunch by sprinkling over it rolled oats, grated cheese, or crushed savoury biscuits.

SALADS

A few years ago salad meant little more than floppy, soggy lettuce leaves with perhaps a few slices of watery tomato and limp cucumber, but now the word covers such a wide variety of dishes (e.g. crisp green salads, cooked salads, cool salads with warm dressings, couscous-based salads, salads with meat, vegetarian salads with fruit and nuts or seeds, salads made crunchy by the addition of croutons . . .), that I find that I eat a lot of salads, sometimes planned in advance, other times created to use ingredients I have to hand. Salads have many roles – as first courses, snacks, light meals, accompaniments or meals in themselves, and they are the easiest of dishes to make, and to improvise. Composition, quantities and flavourings are invariably open to modification, and can be scaled up or down to suit the occasion.

Most of the salads here are suitable for any occasion, depending on your appetite and what else is on offer. The exceptions are those that contain meat or fish, which may not be suitable as main-course accompaniments.

Tomato and Roquefort Salad

If I am only able to use tomatoes that have very little flavour and Roquefort from a sealed packet I do not bother to make this salad, as I know how wonderful it can taste when made with richly flavoured sun-ripened tomatoes, and Roquefort freshly cut from a large piece.

2 large, well-flavoured
    tomatoes, chopped
30g/1oz Roquefort cheese
1 tablespoon walnut oil

½ teaspoon sherry vinegar
black pepper
roughly chopped walnuts
chopped fresh parsley

Put the chopped tomatoes into a bowl then crumble the Roquefort over. Beat the oil into the vinegar, pour this over the cheese and tomatoes and sprinkle black pepper over. Finish with a scattering of chopped walnuts and parsley.

—— *Red Pepper and Anchovy Salad* ——

1 medium red pepper
1 anchovy fillet, soaked,
    drained and cut lengthways
    into fine strips
2–3 large black olives, stoned
    and sliced

finely chopped parsley
2 tablespoons extra-virgin
    olive oil
warm crusty bread, to serve

Skin the red pepper by placing it under a very hot grill, turning occasionally, until blistered all over and burnt black in places – this usually takes about 15–20 minutes. Alternatively, spear the pepper with a fork then hold it over a flame until it is evenly charred. When the pepper is cool enough to handle cut away the stem and discard the seeds. Rub off the charred patches then, using a vegetable knife, scrape away the rest of the skin. If necessary, rinse very briefly under cold running water.

Cut the flesh into strips and place in a shallow serving dish. Scatter the anchovy fillet, olives and parsley over then drizzle the olive oil over. Cover and leave in the refrigerator for about 8–12 hours.

Serve at room temperature with warm crusty bread to mop up the juices.

Cauliflower Tonnato

approximately 175g/6oz cauliflower florets

salt and freshly ground black pepper

half a 100g/3½oz can tuna fish, drained

1 tablespoon mayonnaise

1 tablespoon plain yogurt

1½ teaspoons capers

2 large green olives, stoned

1 tablespoon parsley leaves

approximately ¼ teaspoon green peppercorn paste (optional)

lemon juice

freshly ground black pepper

1 anchovy fillet, soaked in a little milk

finely chopped parsley, for garnish

Steam the cauliflower over salted water until just tender.

Meanwhile, mix together the tuna fish, mayonnaise, yogurt, capers, olives, parsley and green peppercorn paste, if using, and add lemon juice and black pepper to taste. Heat through gently, preferably in a nonstick pan, stirring; do not allow to boil.

Drain the anchovy fillet and cut into thin lengthways strips.

Place the cauliflower in a warmed bowl, pour the warm sauce over, toss lightly and scatter the anchovy strips and parsley over the top.

VARIATIONS
- Blend approximately ¼ teaspoon anchovy purée or paste into the sauce instead of using an anchovy fillet.
- Flavour the mayonnaise with Tabasco sauce or tomato purée.
- Scatter sliced olives over with the anchovy and parsley.

Cauliflower with Prawns

The other half of the cauliflower can be used for a soup (see page 15), to make a purée (see page 105), or for the recipes on pages 53 and 115.

½ small head cauliflower florets (approximately 115g/4oz)
1 tablespoon soured cream

freshly ground black pepper and creamed horseradish
approximately 55g/2oz prawns
grated lemon rind

Steam the cauliflower over boiling salted water until just tender. Meanwhile, mix the soured cream with the black pepper and horseradish. Toss the cauliflower and prawns together, pour the soured cream over and toss again. Sprinkle some shreds of grated lemon rind over. Serve hot or warm.

VARIATION
● Sprinkle with a few lightly toasted flaked almonds.

Broccoli and Red Pepper Salad

approximately 115g/4oz broccoli
1 tablespoon extra-virgin olive oil
1 teaspoon tarragon vinegar
salt and freshly ground black pepper
1 small red pepper, grilled (see

page 50), skinned and thinly sliced
2–3 black olives, stoned
1 heaped teaspoon capers
1 teaspoon fresh parsley, chopped
pinch chopped fresh thyme

Trim off the tough parts of the broccoli stalks then pare away the thick fibrous skin. Cut the stalks diagonally into slices approximately 0.5cm/¼in thick. Steam the sliced stalks and florets over boiling salted water until just tender. Refresh under cold running water then drain well.

Mix together the oil, vinegar and seasoning. Toss the broccoli, red pepper, olives, capers and herbs together, pour the dressing over then toss again.

VARIATION

- Make a more substantial salad by adding 40–55g/1½–2oz cheese, such as goat's cheese or Feta, which would continue the overall salty, piquant theme, redolent of Greece (I would omit the salt in the dressing), or add a more creamy cheese for a contrast.

———— *Cauliflower and Broccoli Salad* ————

85g/3oz trimmed cauliflower florets
55g/2oz trimmed broccoli florets
2 small sprigs fresh mint
1½ teaspoons white wine vinegar
½ teaspoon grain herb mustard
1 tablespoon extra-virgin olive oil
1 small clove garlic, crushed (optional)
salt and freshly ground black pepper
1½ teaspoons roughly chopped chives

Steam the cauliflower and broccoli with one of the sprigs of mint over boiling salted water for 4–5 minutes or until just tender. Refresh under cold running water then drain well and discard the mint.

Mix the vinegar and mustard together then blend in the oil. Add the garlic, if using, and salt and black pepper to taste. Shred the remaining mint.

Put the vegetables into a bowl, pour the dressing over and toss together.

If time allows, cover and chill for at least 3 hours.

Sprinkle the shredded mint and chives over before serving.

VARIATION
● Use either all cauliflower or all broccoli.

———— *Green Bean and Anchovy Salad* ————

115g/4oz French beans
1–2 anchovy fillets, soaked in
   a little milk for 15 minutes
1 tablespoon virgin olive oil
1½ teaspoons lemon juice
finely grated rind ¼ lemon
freshly ground black pepper
½ small clove garlic, crushed
finely chopped chives or
   parsley

Boil or steam the beans for about 2 minutes so they remain very crisp. Drain; if boiled, refresh under cold running water then drain well.

Drain the anchovies, gently pat them dry, then cut into long thin strips.

Whisk the oil and lemon juice together then add the lemon rind and freshly ground black pepper.

Rub a small salad bowl with the garlic clove. Put the beans and anchovies into the bowl then toss with the dressing. Scatter chopped chives or parsley over.

VARIATION
● Add some crisp garlic croutons.

Chicory with Hazelnut Dressing

a little milk
approximately 30g/1oz soft
  cheese
scant tablespoon crushed
  lightly toasted hazelnuts
lemon juice

salt and freshly ground black
  pepper
1 small chicory head
fresh chervil, coriander or
  parsley

Blend a little milk into the cheese to 'loosen' it. Add the hazelnuts, lemon juice and seasoning to taste.

Chop the chicory and put into a bowl. Spoon over the dressing, toss lightly and sprinkle with the chervil, coriander or parsley.

VARIATION
● Add a little hazelnut oil to the dressing.

Melon with Prosciutto

The flesh of both Ogen and Charentais melons is sweet and juicy, which makes a good counterbalance to the ham. For serving suggestions for the other half of the melon, see page 211, or use in Prawns with Mint and Melon (see page 148).

½ Ogen or Charentais melon,
  seeds removed
1 slice prosciutto crudo, e.g.
  Parma ham, cut into strips
1 tablespoon lime juice

1½ teaspoons extra-virgin
  olive oil
salt and freshly ground black
  pepper
leaves from a small sprig of
  mint, shredded

Scoop out the flesh from the melon, using a melon baller or teaspoon. Toss with the strips of ham.

Mix the lime juice, oil and seasoning together, pour over the melon and ham then add the mint and toss together lightly. Serve immediately.

VARIATION
● Melon with Prawns — use 55g/2oz prawns instead of the prosciutto.

_____ *Duck Crackling Salad with Orange* _____
Sesame Vinaigrette

1½ teaspoons mild olive oil
skin of ½ duck breast or 1
    small duck breast, cut into
    thin strips
1 tablespoon orange juice
salt and freshly ground black
    pepper

½ teaspoon sesame oil
small salad leaves, such as
    curly endive, or small
    spinach leaves
watercress leaves (if not using
    spinach leaves)
toasted sesame seeds

Heat ½ teaspoon of the olive oil in a small, heavy frying pan, add the duck skin and cook over a low heat until crisp. Blot off excess oil with absorbent paper.

Meanwhile blend the orange juice and seasoning together in a small bowl then slowly beat in the sesame oil and remaining olive oil. Adjust the proportions of the various ingredients to get the balance that you like.

Put the salad leaves into a bowl, pour the dressing over and toss together. Sprinkle a little salt on the duck skin then scatter the skin and sesame seeds over the salad.

VARIATION
● Substitute chicken skin for duck.

Tuna and Flageolet Bean Salad

If using freshly cooked beans, toss them in the dressing whilst still warm then leave to cool before adding the remaining salad ingredients. If using canned flageolet beans, rinse them after draining to remove all traces of the canning liquid.

2 tablespoons virgin or extra-virgin olive oil

1 clove garlic, crushed

approximately 2 teaspoons lemon juice

salt and freshly ground black pepper

100g/3½oz can tuna

approximately 85g/3oz cooked or drained flageolet beans

1–2 teaspoons chopped capers

1 or 2 spring onions, thinly sliced

oak leaf or other crisp lettuce (optional)

chopped fresh parsley

Whisk together the oil, garlic, lemon juice and seasoning. Lightly toss together the tuna, drained if preferred, the beans, capers and spring onion. Mix in the dressing, then chill lightly.

Serve on a bed of crisp lettuce leaves, if liked, and with plenty of chopped parsley sprinkled over.

VARIATION
• Substitute cannellini beans for flageolet beans.

Bulgur Salads

Bulgur, or burghul as it is also known, is boiled wheat that has been dried to a paste then ground. This means it needs no further cooking, just a little moistening, and it makes a foolproof, amazingly adaptable base for warm and cold salads.

Cold Bulgur Salads

For 1 first-course portion:

30g/1oz bulgur
150ml/5fl oz water or stock
approximately 1½ tablespoons
   olive oil
approximately 1½ tablespoons
   lemon juice
salt and freshly ground black
   pepper

Soak the bulgur in cold water or stock for about 15 minutes so that it still retains a slight 'bite', stirring occasionally. Tip the bulgur into a sieve and press out as much liquid as possible. Mix the oil and lemon juice together, pour half over the bulgur, add seasoning and stir to mix. If time allows leave to soak for an hour. Stir in the remaining dressing and the chosen ingredients – some can be sprinkled over the top. Serve at room temperature, not from the refrigerator.

Suggested additional
   ingredients include:
chopped fresh chives, mint or
   coriander
chopped garlic
stoned and quartered black
   olives
skinned, seeded and chopped
   tomatoes
chopped anchovy fillets
quartered hard-boiled egg

flaked, drained tuna fish
flaked cooked fish
chopped cooked meat
nuts
toasted seeds
Middle Eastern Tabbouleh –
   add chopped spring onions,
   skinned, seeded tomatoes
   and plenty of finely chopped
   parsley with half as much
   mint

Warm Bulgur Salads

The bulgur can either be fried first, or, for a lighter dish, either about 15g/½oz butter, or 1 tablespoon olive oil, can be stirred into the cooked bulgur.

For 1 main-course portion:

knob unsalted butter	55g/2oz bulgur
1½ teaspoons olive oil	70ml/2½fl oz hot stock or
1 small shallot, chopped	water

Heat the butter and oil, add the shallot and cook gently until softened. Stir in the bulgur and heat gently, stirring, until golden brown. Add the stock or water, stir once then leave over a very low heat for a few minutes until the liquid has been absorbed. Either eat straight away whilst the grains still have some bite, or cover and leave to soften.

VARIATIONS
- Use a nut oil.
- Add some chopped herbs.
- Middle Eastern Bulgur Salad – add cumin, coriander or cardamom seeds or cloves when cooking the shallot and scatter over the top raisins, almonds and chopped dried apricots, all of which have been lightly fried in butter; finish with a light sprinkling of cinnamon.
- Oriental Bulgur Salad – sprinkle a little sesame oil and some toasted sesame seeds over.
- Cheese Bulgur Salad – stir through a tasty cheese that melts readily, such as Gruyère, Emmenthal, Halloumi, or goat's- or ewe's-milk cheeses. Finish with some chopped sun-dried tomatoes, if liked.
- Cumin and Tomato Bulgur Salad – heat a small pinch of cumin seeds in a heavy pan until they turn colour and pop. Add to 2 tablespoons French dressing flavoured with a little garlic and a small pinch of paprika then mix with approximately 40–55g/1½–2oz bulgur, ½ a diced small red pepper, a chopped and seeded tomato and about 4 stoned and halved black olives.

Lentil Salad with Walnuts

Depending on the size of your appetite, this salad can be a first course, a snack or the main course of a light meal.

approximately 1 tablespoon double cream or Greek yogurt

approximately 1½ tablespoons olive oil

½ tablespoon walnut oil

lemon juice, white wine vinegar or tarragon vinegar, to taste

salt and freshly ground black pepper

approximately 85g/3oz cooked green lentils

1 shallot or 1 large spring onion, finely chopped

approximately 1 tablespoon chopped fresh coriander or parsley

lettuce leaves

approximately 1–1½ tablespoons chopped walnuts

Mix the cream or yogurt with the oils then add lemon juice or vinegar and seasoning, adjusting to taste. Toss together the lentils, shallot or spring onion and coriander or parsley. Pour the dressing over and toss briefly again. Serve on a bed of lettuce leaves, with the nuts scattered over.

VARIATION
• Make the salad more substantial by adding some drained canned tuna or crab, diced tongue or ham or chopped grilled or fried bacon.

Lentil, Feta and Red Pepper Salad

approximately 55–85g/2–3 oz cooked green lentils
1 tablespoon lemon juice
small pinch each paprika and cayenne pepper
1 small clove garlic, finely crushed
olive oil
1 small red pepper, roasted (see page 50) and cut into strips
½ teaspoon chopped fresh mint
2 teaspoons chopped mixed fresh herbs – parsley, marjoram, thyme
salt and freshly ground pepper
55g/2oz Feta cheese or crumbly goat's cheese

Warm the lentils. Mix together the lemon juice, paprika, cayenne, garlic and 2 tablespoons olive oil then stir into the lentils with most of the red pepper, the mint, herbs and seasoning. Crumble the cheese and stir into the lentil mixture. Serve with the remaining red pepper scattered over the top and a little more olive oil poured over.

VARIATION

- Green Lentil and Sausage Salad – cook a finely chopped shallot in a little oil until softened then stir in 2 teaspoons white wine vinegar, a pinch of caraway seeds and a couple of teaspoons of tarragon mustard. Mix together the lentils, red pepper and about 40g/1½oz thinly sliced smoked sausage. Pour over the dressing, season to taste and eat warm or cold.

SERVES ONE

Wilted Spinach Salad

3 tablespoons olive oil
1 clove garlic, finely crushed
2 slices baguette
approximately 85–115g/
    3–4oz young spinach
2–3 spring onions, thickly
    sliced

4 large black olives, stoned
    and quartered
1½ teaspoons tarragon
    vinegar
55g/2oz Feta cheese

Mix the olive oil and garlic together. Brush both sides of the bread with some of the oil then bake at 200°C/400°F/gas mark 6 for 6–8 minutes, or place under a moderate grill, until browned and crisp. Cut into small squares to make croutons. Tear large spinach leaves into two or three pieces but leave small ones whole. Put all the leaves into a serving bowl and toss with the spring onions and olives. Crumble the cheese over. Heat the remaining oil until it is very hot but not quite smoking. Pour it over the spinach immediately and toss the leaves so that as many as possible are wilted. Scatter the croutons over and eat immediately.

VARIATIONS
- I like to make a strong, creamy mustard dressing for this salad. Mix a scant teaspoon tarragon vinegar with 2 teaspoons wholegrain mustard and 1 tablespoon crème fraîche, soured cream or Greek yogurt then gradually whisk in 2 tablespoons extra-virgin olive oil to make a thick sauce.
- Alternatively, gently heat in a nonstick pan some Tarragon and Mustard Mayonnaise (see page 238), or plain mayonnaise flavoured with mustard, and pour over the salad.
- Substitute 1 small head endive for the spinach.

Warm Red Cabbage Salad

For recipes using the other half of the cabbage see pages 183 and 208.

1 rasher bacon, chopped	2 teaspoons sherry vinegar
1 tablespoon olive oil	½ teaspoon Dijon mustard
30g/1oz walnut halves	salt and freshly ground black
½ small red cabbage (about	pepper
85–115g/3–4oz), shredded	

Cook the bacon in a heavy, preferably nonstick, pan until crisp. Using a slotted spoon, transfer the bacon to absorbent kitchen paper to drain. Add the oil to the pan, heat through then stir in the nuts and cook, stirring occasionally, until brittle. Using a slotted spoon, transfer to absorbent paper, pour the oil from the pan and reserve.

Meanwhile, blanch the cabbage for 1–2 minutes in boiling salted water. Drain, refresh in cold running water then drain well. Put into a bowl and scatter the nuts and bacon over.

Stir the vinegar and mustard into the pan used for cooking the nuts and bacon, bring to the boil then gradually whisk in the reserved oil. Add seasoning to taste, pour the dressing over the cabbage and toss briefly.

VARIATIONS
- Add 1 diced small apple or pear, or ½ a larger one.
- Add about 4 stoned and halved no-soak prunes.

Warm Endive and Smoked Bacon Salad

1 rasher smoked bacon,
  chopped
1–2 slices baguette, or 1 small
  slice bread, crusts removed,
  cubed
olive oil, for cooking

2 teaspoons white wine
  vinegar
1 small clove garlic, crushed
Dijon mustard, salt and freshly
  ground black pepper
small head curly endive

Cook the bacon in a small, preferably nonstick, pan until the fat
runs. Using a slotted spoon, transfer to absorbent kitchen paper
and keep warm. Stir the bread cubes into the pan and cook,
turning occasionally, until crisp and brown; add olive oil as
necessary. Remove using a slotted spoon and keep warm.

For the dressing you will need about 1 tablespoon oil in the
pan, so either add more or tip out any excess. Stir the vinegar,
garlic, mustard and seasoning into the oil, and heat but do not
boil. Remove the garlic. Pour the dressing over the endive, toss
to coat then sprinkle the bacon and croutons over.

VARIATIONS
- Warm Endive and Chicken Liver Salad – lightly fry approximately 55g/2oz chicken livers in the fat from the bacon, then
  keep warm with the bacon. Use red wine, balsamic or sherry
  vinegar to make the dressing.
- Instead of croutons, add some chopped lightly toasted hazelnuts, walnuts, pine nuts or sunflower seeds to the main recipe
  or any of the variations.
- Endive and Stilton Salad – omit the bacon, prepare a dressing
  by mixing together 15g/½oz Stilton, 1½ tablespoons olive oil,
  1½ teaspoons crème fraîche, soured cream or Greek yogurt, 1
  teaspoon sherry vinegar or lemon juice, a touch of Dijon
  mustard, and black pepper. Toss with the salad leaves and
  croutons then scatter a little more chopped Stilton over.

- Use chicory leaves and some watercress leaves instead of the endive.
- Substitute spinach for the endive in the main recipe or any of the variations.

Warm Cabbage Salad with Grapes and Caraway Seeds

1 small onion, finely chopped
olive oil, for cooking
pinch of caraway seeds
½ small white cabbage, thinly shredded

2 tablespoons medium-bodied dry white wine (optional)
55g/2oz seedless green grapes, halved if large
salt and freshly ground black pepper

Gently cook the onion in a little olive oil until softened, then stir in the caraway seeds followed by the cabbage and wine, if using. Stir until the cabbage is coated with oil then cover and cook, shaking the pan occasionally, for about 10 minutes so the cabbage retains some 'bite'. Stir in the grapes and cook uncovered for 2–3 minutes. Add salt and pepper to taste then serve with the cooking juices spooned over.

VARIATIONS
- Cook a chopped rasher of bacon with the onion, and omit the grapes.
- Add ½ a diced apple or pear with the cabbage and omit the grapes.
- Substitute 2 or 3 crushed juniper berries or a pinch of cumin seeds for the caraway seeds in the main recipe or any of the variations.

Warm Potato, Bacon and _____
Watercress Salad

This salad is substantial enough for a satisfying lunch or supper dish.

approximately 100g/3½oz
 small new potatoes,
 unpeeled
1 rasher streaky bacon,
 coarsely chopped
55g/2oz watercress, trimmed
1½ teaspoons mild olive or
 sunflower oil

2 teaspoons white wine
 vinegar
salt, freshly ground black
 pepper
wholegrain or tarragon
 mustard

Steam the new potatoes over boiling water until just tender. Meanwhile, cook the bacon in a small, heavy frying pan until it is crisp and the fat runs.

When the potatoes are cooked, remove them from the heat and cut into slices whilst still hot. Put into a bowl with the watercress. Using a slotted spoon, transfer the bacon from the frying pan to the bowl. Quickly stir the oil, vinegar, seasoning and a little mustard into the bacon fat and bring to the boil. Pour into the bowl and toss all the ingredients together.

Celeriac and Gammon Salad

1 teaspoon golden mustard
   seeds
¼ teaspoon Dijon mustard
1 tablespoon sherry vinegar
3 tablespoons fromage blanc
salt
½ small head celeriac

1 tablespoon lemon juice
approximately 55g/2oz cooked
   gammon
1 tomato, preferably skinned,
   chopped
55g/2oz watercress, trimmed

Heat the mustard seeds in a small, heavy pan for a few seconds until they begin to pop. Transfer to a bowl then mix in the Dijon mustard, vinegar and fromage blanc. Add salt to taste.

Peel the celeriac then cut into fine shreds. Toss immediately in the lemon juice then mix with the gammon, tomato and watercress. Pour over the mustard dressing and toss lightly.

VARIATIONS
- If you do not have any mustard seeds, use wholegrain mustard instead of Dijon, although the flavour will not be the same.
- Cooked bacon, cooked ham, or raw ham such as Parma, can be used in place of gammon.
- Use some drained, canned smoked oysters or mussels instead of the gammon.

Smoked Mackerel and New Potato Salad

It is best to start the preparation for this salad about a couple of hours in advance so the potatoes absorb the flavours of the dressing. Serve as a main course.

115g/4oz new potatoes, unpeeled

1 tablespoon olive oil

2 teaspoons white wine vinegar

2 teaspoons horseradish sauce, or to taste

salt and freshly ground black pepper

3.75cm/1½in piece cucumber (optional)

85–115g/3–4oz smoked mackerel fillet, skinned

½ crisp apple

1 tablespoon soured cream

lettuce

Steam the potatoes until tender. Meanwhile whisk together the oil, vinegar, horseradish and seasoning. Halve or slice the potatoes if necessary then immediately stir into the dressing. Leave to cool, stirring occasionally.

If using the cucumber, cut it in half, remove the seeds, and cut the flesh into small chunks. Place in a colander, sprinkle with salt and leave for about 30 minutes. Rinse, drain and pat dry on absorbent paper.

Skin the mackerel then break the flesh into chunks. Chop the apple. Gently fold together all the ingredients, including the soured cream, taking care not to break up the fish. Serve on a bed of lettuce.

VARIATION
- Substitute smoked oysters or smoked mussels for the mackerel.

EGGS

Omelettes

Some people can become amazingly animated and dogmatic on the subject of making omelettes, with very firm views on whether cream, milk or water should be added. Each addition changes the character of the omelette slightly, and it is a matter of taste how set or liquid you prefer the centre to be. There are some general points, though, for making successful omelettes. Beat the eggs until they are just broken and the whites and yolks mixed; pour the eggs quickly into hot butter or oil then, over a fairly high heat, twirl the pan once or twice, at the same time using a wooden spatula or a fork to bring the cooking egg mixture from the sides to the centre of the pan in a long sweep, allowing the uncooked egg to flow on to the hot surface. Cooking should be completed quickly, and immediately the edge nearest you is just set, fold it over, using the side of a fork. Tip the pan up, roll the omelette down, then tip it sharply on to a warmed plate.

Fillings for omelettes are legion, and here are just a few suggestions – cheese, of course (see page 72); finely chopped fresh herbs (add a little grated Parmesan to the egg mixture when using chives); chopped, seasoned diced tomato; cauliflower mixed with seasoned cream, fromage frais or Greek yogurt plus a little grated nutmeg; broccoli or leeks; diced ham or tongue heated through with seasoned cream or fromage frais flavoured with horseradish; lightly sautéed mushrooms with herbs; Ratatouille (see page 109); Peperonata (see page 109); potted shrimps or prawns.

Courgette Omelette

Leaving the courgette with salt sprinkled over draws out excess moisture, a process known as 'degorging'.

1 small–medium firm
  courgette, coarsely grated
salt
olive oil
2 eggs
1 tablespoon double cream,
  fromage blanc or quark

pinch chopped fresh marjoram
  or tarragon
freshly ground black pepper
freshly grated Parmesan
  cheese

Layer the courgette in a colander with salt sprinkled over each layer and leave for about 30–60 minutes. Press down well on the courgette to extract as much water as possible then dry on absorbent paper.

Heat a little oil in a small, nonstick frying pan, add the courgette and cook over a fairly high heat, stirring frequently, for 6–7 minutes.

Meanwhile, lightly beat the eggs with the cream, fromage blanc or quark, the herb and black pepper. Reduce the heat beneath the courgette to moderate, pour in the eggs and cook until lightly set on top. Sprinkle a little Parmesan over and roll the omelette up.

VARIATION
• Add a little finely grated Parmesan to the egg mixture instead of the cream, fromage blanc or quark, and stir a spoonful or so of cream or fromage blanc into the courgette.

Smoked Salmon and Dill Omelette Slices

This tastes and sounds luxurious, but it need not be expensive if smoked salmon trimmings are used.

knob unsalted butter
2 eggs
salt and freshly ground black
   pepper

30–40g/1–1½oz smoked
   salmon trimmings
1 tablespoon chopped fresh
   dill, or pinch dried dill

Heat the butter in an omelette pan. Lightly beat the eggs together and add black pepper and just a little salt. Pour into the pan and cook over a high heat for about a minute, drawing a wooden spatula through the mixture to allow the uncooked egg to cover the surface of the pan. Roughly chop about a third of the smoked salmon and sprinkle over the omelette with the dill. Fold the omelette into three and flip on to a warmed plate. Cut across into slices. Arrange the remaining salmon on a serving plate and place the omelette strips on top. Garnish with sprigs of dill.

VARIATIONS
- Substitute prawns or cold-smoked trout for the salmon.
- Try a different herb e.g. fennel, chives or basil.

Crab Omelette

I like the contrast of the cool, creamy filling with the warm omelette, but if you prefer the filling to be hot it can be warmed gently in a small saucepan; do not allow it to boil.

I prefer to use fresh crabmeat because of its superior flavour and texture, but often it really is more practical to use thawed frozen crab, or even crab sticks.

1 spring onion, finely chopped
1 ½–2 tablespoons fromage
   blanc, Greek yogurt or
   soured cream
55g;/2oz cooked crabmeat,
thawed frozen crab or crab
   sticks, chopped
salt, freshly ground black
   pepper and paprika
2 eggs, lightly beaten

Mix the spring onion with the fromage blanc, yogurt or soured cream. Add the crab, or crab sticks, and season to taste with salt, pepper and paprika.

Make the omelette. While the top is still moist, spoon on the crab mixture, cook for a minute or so then fold the omelette over and serve.

VARIATIONS
- Add extra bite to the filling with a dash of Tabasco sauce.
- Substitute chopped prawns for the crab.

Cheese Omelettes

The only omelettes I ate when I was young were cheese ones, and they are still my favourites. I never tire of them, because I don't restrict them to just one or two cheeses, such as Cheddar or Parmesan, but am always discovering delicious new tastes by making omelettes with different cheeses – Brie, Maroilles, Fourme d'Ambert, goat's cheese – or a combination of cheeses, such as Parmesan and Brie. Try grating the cheese so that it melts, shredding or chopping it so that it only partially melts, and adding it to the eggs, sprinkled over the top of the omelette before rolling it up, or adding half to the beaten eggs and using the remainder as the filling. Another method is to melt the cheese gently in a saucepan with a little milk or cream, then pour it over a lightly set plain omelette.

An omelette is only as good, though, as the quality of the cheese. The character of the omelette can also be changed by adding other flavourings, such as herbs and seasonings – try Tabasco sauce, mustard or horseradish sauce.

Crouton, Blue Brie and Walnut Omelette

Crisp walnuts, crunchy croutons and sharp, soft cheese are combined inside the omelette. Very 'moreish'.

1 slice French bread, or small slice bread, crusts removed
1–1½ tablespoons walnut oil
2 walnut halves, roughly chopped

2 eggs
salt and freshly ground black pepper
30g/1oz blue Brie or Cambozola cheese, rind removed, chopped

Cut the bread into small cubes then fry in a little hot walnut oil until crisp. Using a slotted spoon, transfer to absorbent kitchen paper to drain. Fry the walnuts in the hot oil until brown then transfer to absorbent paper. Lightly whisk the eggs, season with a little salt and plenty of black pepper then pour into the hot oil and make an omelette, scattering over the cheese, croutons and nuts while the top is still soft. Fold over, transfer to a warmed plate and leave for a moment to allow the cheese to melt slightly.

Courgette Eggahs

1 small–medium courgette, thinly sliced or shredded
salt
olive oil
1 shallot, finely chopped

1 small clove garlic, crushed
2 eggs, separated
1 teaspoon finely chopped fresh tarragon
freshly ground black pepper

Put the courgette into a colander, sprinkling salt between the layers, and leave for about 30–60 minutes. Press down well on the courgette to extract as much moisture as possible then pat dry on absorbent kitchen paper. Heat a little oil in a small frying pan, add the shallot and garlic and cook until softened but not coloured. Remove from the pan and drain on absorbent kitchen paper. Cook the courgette in the pan, stirring occasionally, until soft then remove and drain on absorbent paper. Tip the courgette into a bowl, mash to a purée then beat in the egg yolks, tarragon, shallot, garlic, black pepper and salt. Whisk the egg whites until stiff and lightly fold into the courgette mixture until just evenly blended.

Drop spoonfuls of the courgette mixture into hot oil, spread out each dollop of mixture and cook until golden on both sides, turning once.

VARIATION

• Flavour the mixture with marjoram and a pinch of nutmeg instead of tarragon.

Asparagus Frittata

Frittatas are cooked more slowly than omelettes – traditionally until they are set but not solid, but I prefer to leave them slightly liquid in the centre and therefore lighter.

115g/4oz asparagus, trimmed
2 eggs
2 tablespoons freshly grated Parmesan cheese

salt and freshly ground black pepper
small knob unsalted butter

Place the thicker parts of the asparagus in a steaming basket or colander, cover and steam over gently boiling seasoned water for about 5 minutes. Add the thinner stems and steam for a further

5 minutes or so – the thickness of asparagus stems, and therefore the cooking time, can vary quite a lot so do check them as they cook.

Chop the asparagus. Beat the eggs until the yolks and whites are just blended then add the asparagus, Parmesan and seasoning.

Heat the butter over a moderate heat in a fairly heavy nonstick frying pan. Pour in the egg mixture, lower the heat and cook slowly until the eggs are lightly set almost completely throughout with just the top still moist. Flash under a hot grill, if liked, to lightly brown the top.

Slide on to a warm serving plate.

Brie and Bacon Egg Roll

55g/2oz Ricotta, curd or sieved cottage cheese
2 teaspoons finely grated Parmesan cheese
1 tablespoon Greek yogurt or fromage blanc
1 egg, separated
freshly ground black pepper
unsalted butter
1 small bacon rasher, chopped
1 spring onion or small shallot, chopped
approximately 30–40g/ 1–1½oz Brie without rind, chopped
chopped fresh parsley

Stir the Ricotta, curd or cottage cheese, Parmesan, yogurt or fromage blanc and egg yolk together. Season with freshly ground black pepper.

Whisk the egg white until stiff but not dry then fold lightly into the egg yolk mixture until just evenly mixed.

Heat a little unsalted butter in a frying pan or omelette pan, add the egg mixture and gently smooth it out until even. Cook over a moderately low heat until just set throughout.

Meanwhile in a separate pan cook the bacon with the onion or shallot in a little butter until the shallot has softened. Remove from the heat, briefly and lightly stir in the Brie then spoon this over the egg mixture. Sprinkle with parsley and black pepper then roll up.

VARIATION
● Substitute Camembert, goat's or ewe's cheese for the Brie.

----------------- *Feta and Olive Roll* -----------------

If I have some taramasalata in the fridge I thin it down with a little yogurt to make a sauce to serve with this roll.

generous 30g/1oz Feta cheese, grated
1 egg, separated
1 teaspoon crème fraîche, soured cream or double cream
freshly ground black pepper

oil, for frying
scant 30g/1oz stoned black olives, finely chopped
1½ tablespoons mayonnaise
1 tablespoon freshly grated Parmesan cheese
tomato slices

Mix the Feta cheese with the egg yolk, crème fraîche or double cream and season with black pepper. Whisk the egg white until stiff but not dry. Fold a little of the cheese mixture into the egg white then gently fold in the remainder until just evenly blended.

Heat a little oil in a large, preferably nonstick, frying pan, pour in the egg mixture, spreading it in a thin, even layer, and cook over a moderate heat until the centre is just firm. Meanwhile, mix the olives and mayonnaise together.

Spread the olive mixture evenly over the omelette, roll up and sprinkle with Parmesan. Place briefly under a hot grill, if liked, to brown.

Cut into slices and eat with tomato slices.

Poached Eggs in Lettuce

It is preferable to use eggs at room temperature, but if you do use them straight from the refrigerator, allow a little more cooking time.

2 eggs   3–4 tablespoons mayonnaise
2 lettuce leaves   seed mustard

Poach the eggs in an egg poacher, or by slipping them very carefully into a shallow pan of barely simmering salted water then cooking gently for about 3–4 minutes until the yolks are lightly set.

Meanwhile, plunge the lettuce leaves into boiling water, remove, rinse under cold running water then gently pat dry. Heat the mayonnaise in a small bowl placed over a saucepan of hot water.

Spread out the leaves, which will have curled up. Put a poached egg yolk-side downwards in the centre of each lettuce leaf, fold the leaves over then turn the packages over and place on a warmed plate. Add seed mustard to the mayonnaise to taste then spoon on top of the lettuce.

VARIATIONS
- Place a small spoonful of chopped sautéed mushrooms or peppers on the lettuce beneath the eggs.
- Place a little pesto, anchovy paste, or soft cheese with herbs or garlic and herbs on the lettuce beneath the eggs.
- Serve on toast or on a bed of vegetable purée.
- Flavour the mayonnaise with just a pinch of curry powder, horseradish, or finely chopped fresh herbs such as chives, tarragon or chervil.

Poached Egg with Pea and Lettuce Purée

unsalted butter
1 shallot, finely chopped
2 lettuce leaves, shredded
55g/2oz frozen petits pois
approximately 1 tablespoon
 chopped fresh parsley

1 ½ tablespoons chicken or
 vegetable stock (optional)
1 ½ tablespoons Greek yogurt,
 fromage blanc or milk
salt and freshly ground black
 pepper
2 eggs

Heat a little butter in a small saucepan, add the shallot and cook until softened, shaking the pan occasionally. Add the shredded lettuce and cook for a few minutes until softened then stir in the peas, parsley, and stock if using, or an equivalent amount of water plus a pinch of salt. Cover with a circle of greaseproof paper then put the lid on the pan and cook over a low heat until the peas are tender. Remove a few of the peas and set aside. Add the yogurt, fromage blanc or milk to the pan then purée the mixture to give the consistency of a thick vegetable soup. Add seasoning and reheat gently.

 Meanwhile, poach the eggs for 3–4 minutes so the yolks remain soft. Spoon the purée on to a plate and top with the eggs. Scatter the reserved peas over. The egg yolks should bathe the purée in a warm, golden sauce when pierced.

VARIATIONS
- Add mayonnaise to the purée instead of yogurt, fromage blanc or milk.
- Serve on a slice of toasted country-style bread, or on noodles.
- Spoon over a sauce of warmed mayonnaise, Aïoli (see page 239), or seasoned fromage blanc, crème fraîche or Greek yogurt.

Poached Egg on Soffrito

This rich-tasting tomato and onion mixture is also good with scrambled eggs – add the raw eggs to the cooked vegetables and stir together over a low heat until the eggs are lightly set.

fruity olive oil
2 shallots or 1 small onion, finely chopped
approximately 1–1½ teaspoons paprika, to taste
1 small clove garlic, crushed
4 medium tomatoes, skinned and chopped

2 eggs
2 slices country bread
salt and freshly ground black pepper
1–1½ tablespoons chopped fresh parsley
unsalted butter, or olive oil for spreading on the toast

Heat the oil in a heavy nonstick pan. Add the shallots or onion and cook, stirring occasionally, until softened. Stir in the paprika, cook for a minute or so then stir in the garlic and tomatoes. Cook until reduced to a rich, thick purée.

Meanwhile, poach the eggs for 3–4 minutes and toast the bread.

Season the tomato mixture and stir in most of the parsley.

Spread the hot toast with butter or olive oil, spoon on the tomato mixture and top with the eggs. Scatter a little more parsley over.

VARIATIONS
- Include some diced red pepper in the tomato mixture.
- Spread the buttered or oiled toast with a little anchovy paste, or use soured cream, fromage blanc or a soft cheese (a soft goat's cheese makes a very tasty dish) instead of butter or oil.
- Substitute fresh basil or tarragon for parsley.

Spinach Egg

350g/12oz fresh spinach, trimmed (or about 225g/8oz frozen, thawed)

salt and freshly ground black pepper

15g/½oz unsalted butter

1 small clove garlic, finely crushed

2 eggs

55g/2oz Feta cheese, crumbled

2 spring onions, finely sliced (optional)

Wash the fresh spinach and leave the excess moisture on the leaves. Tear the leaves and cook in a covered saucepan over a moderate heat for about 5 minutes, shaking the pan occasionally. Uncover, stir, and cook until excess moisture has evaporated. Tip into a sieve and squeeze out any remaining moisture.

If using thawed frozen spinach, heat it gently in a pan, stirring occasionally, then tip into a sieve and squeeze out excess moisture. Season the spinach well.

Heat the butter, add the garlic and cook briskly for a minute or so, until it begins to sizzle. Stir in the spinach until evenly coated in the butter then, using the back of a wooden spoon, make two hollows in the mixture. Crack the eggs into the hollows, scatter the cheese over, cover with a lid and cook for about 4 minutes or until the eggs are set. Grind black pepper over the eggs and cheese and sprinkle the spring onions, if using, over the whole dish.

VARIATIONS

- Use other cheeses, such as grated Parmesan, goat's or ewe's cheese, or a creamy blue cheese.
- Use strips of anchovy fillet with or instead of the cheese.
- Spinach and Mushroom Egg – use 175g/6oz fresh spinach or 130g/4½oz frozen, and add 55g/2oz sliced mushrooms, cooking them with the garlic.
- Flavour the spinach with grated nutmeg instead of garlic.

Poached Eggs in Leeks

unsalted butter
olive oil
1 shallot, finely chopped
1 small clove garlic, crushed
  (optional)
2 leeks, cut into fine strips
2–3 teaspoons chopped fresh
  parsley

salt and freshly ground black
  pepper
2 eggs
40g/1½oz Gruyère or
  Emmenthal cheese, cut into
  thin slivers

Heat a little butter and olive oil in a frying pan, add the shallot and the garlic, if using, and cook, stirring occasionally, for a few minutes. Add the leeks and cook until they begin to soften.

Stir in the parsley and seasoning then use the back of a wooden spoon to form a hollow in the centre of the mixture. Crack the eggs into the hollow, cover with the cheese then put a lid on the pan. Cook gently for at least 4 minutes until the eggs are just set and the cheese melted. Carefully slide on to a warmed plate, or use a fish slice to remove from the pan.

VARIATIONS
- Use other cheeses, such as sliced Mozzarella, grated Parmesan, crumbled Feta, goat's or ewe's cheese, or a creamy blue cheese.
- Add a dash of walnut oil to the leeks.

Scrambled Eggs

The subject of scrambled eggs arouses almost as much controversy as omelettes. There is no secret to making good, creamy scrambled eggs: all that is needed is a good pan, preferably a nonstick one, a wooden spatula and a *low* heat, so the eggs cook slowly. Lightly beat the eggs with 1 tablespoon cream (or fromage frais or full-fat soft cheese) or water, depending on how light you want the eggs to be. Pour them into a pan containing a little heated butter then cook over a low heat, gently drawing the eggs around the pan as they cook. Do not beat them or stir too briskly. The heat of the pan will continue to cook the eggs after they have been removed from the heat, so lift it away from the stove while the eggs are slightly underdone.

The eggs can be served on toast, in toasted rolls, in Bread Cases (see page 21), on really fresh buttered bread, toasted muffins or crumpets, sautéed or grilled aubergine slices, sautéed or grilled flat or open cup mushrooms, or in a nest of a vegetable purée, such as potato, celeriac, cauliflower or broccoli.

- Useful flavourings for scrambled eggs include chopped fresh herbs, Worcestershire sauce, Tabasco, anchovy purée or paste, mustard (wholegrain is particularly good if the eggs are to accompany bacon), or Anchoïaide (see page 241), Tapenade (see page 240), or pesto, which I prefer to be stirred through the eggs (I will usually add some fromage blanc to the eggs) just before serving, rather than cooked in the pan with the eggs; anchovy fillets can be laid over the cooked eggs.
- The following ingredients can either be added to the eggs while they are cooking, or spooned on to the cooked eggs:
  – buttered or potted shrimps or prawns
  – lightly sautéed mushrooms with dry sherry (optional) stirred into the mushroom cooking juices and boiled to evaporate off then a squeeze of lemon juice and fromage blanc or a soft cheese, perhaps flavoured with herbs and garlic, stirred in
  – chopped sautéed bacon and courgette
  – asparagus tips with a little finely grated Parmesan cheese
  – diced garlic or spicy sausage, diced red pepper and chopped olives
- Scrambled Eggs with Smoked Salmon – just a tablespoon or so of smoked salmon will do (but if you have more, so much the better). Cut it into matchsticks and stir it into creamy

scrambled eggs, just before serving – a real treat. If you have more smoked salmon serve dill-flavoured scrambled eggs on top of thick slices of smoked salmon, or twist smoked salmon slices into a nest and serve the eggs in the centre.

- Try using smoked trout or gravad lax instead of smoked salmon.

- 1 tablespoon seed mustard added to the eggs – this goes well with sweet-cure bacon.

- Stir about 40g/1½oz chopped garlic-and-herb-flavoured soft cheese into the eggs when they are about half set.

- Cheese and Chive Egg – flavour the eggs with a touch of grain mustard, spoon the eggs on to toast then sprinkle over about 30g/1oz finely grated Parmesan or mature Cheddar cheese, followed by some chopped chives and black pepper. Some of the cheese will melt, the rest will stay as fine strands on the surface.

- Spread the toast with mustard, Marmite, anchovy paste or purée, Anchoïaide (see page 241), Tapenade (see page 240), pesto, mayonnaise (tarragon is particularly good) or Aïoli (see page 239); or cover the toast with ham, thinly sliced garlic sausage or spicy sausage.

Simple Soufflés

I often make soufflés, both for myself and when I am cooking for other people, but not the traditional flour-thickened, sauce-based variety. The ones I make are not only far quicker and simpler, they are also much lighter in texture and purer in flavour.

Cheese and Sweetcorn Soufflé

scant 55g/2oz sweetcorn kernels
40g/1½oz soft cheese with garlic and herbs
1 tablespoon Greek yogurt

1 medium egg, separated
salt and freshly ground black pepper
freshly grated Parmesan cheese (optional)

Purée the sweetcorn with the cheese, yogurt, egg yolk and seasoning.

Whisk the egg white until stiff but not dry then lightly fold into the sweetcorn mixture until just evenly blended.

Turn into a buttered ramekin dish approximately 11.5–12.5cm/4½–5in then stand in a steaming basket, colander or large sieve placed over boiling water in a pan, cover with a lid and steam for 12 minutes. Make sure you allow plenty of room for the mixture to rise.

If liked, sprinkle freshly grated Parmesan cheese over the cooked soufflé and place briefly under a preheated hot grill to brown.

Seafood Soufflé

I have called this Seafood Soufflé rather than Crab Soufflé as when I do not want to spend too much I use so-called crab sticks, which are not really crab at all.

40g/1½oz cooked crabmeat, or chopped crab sticks, chilled
1 egg, separated, and 1 egg white

40g/1½oz fromage blanc
1 or 2 drops lemon juice
1 teaspoon paprika
pinch salt

Mix together the crab, egg yolk, fromage blanc, lemon juice, paprika and salt. Whisk the egg white until stiff but not dry, fold a little of the crab mixture into the egg white then gently fold in the remainder until just evenly combined. Spoon into a buttered 7.5cm/3in ramekin dish, place on a baking sheet then bake at 180°C/350°F/gas mark 4 for about 15–17 minutes until just set in the centre. Alternatively steam for about 12 minutes.

VARIATION
- Flavour the soufflé with a pinch of chopped dill, fennel, basil or chervil instead of paprika.

—————————— Leek and Cheese Soufflé ——————————

A light and savoury dish that is especially good when a herb-, garlic- or black peppercorn-flavoured soft cheese is included.

1 small leek, finely chopped
4 tablespoons breadcrumbs
3 tablespoons milk
1 egg, separated
approximately 1 tablespoon
soft cheese – I usually use a flavoured type (optional)
approximately 30g/1oz freshly grated well-flavoured cheese
salt and freshly ground black pepper

Steam the leek or simmer in a little water until tender. Drain, and purée with the breadcrumbs and milk then leave to stand for about 15 minutes. (Alternatively, heat the milk, add the breadcrumbs and leave to soak while the leeks are cooking.)

Add the egg yolk, soft cheese and most of the grated cheese to the leek mixture, then season to taste. Whisk the egg white until stiff but not dry then gently fold into the leek mixture until just evenly blended. Turn into a buttered 10cm/4in ramekin dish, sprinkle over the remaining grated cheese and cook at 180°C/350°F/gas mark 4 for about 25–30 minutes or until lightly set in the centre.

VARIATIONS

- If using a plain soft cheese, add a touch of mustard and/or some chopped chives or parsley.
- Courgette and Cheese Soufflé – in place of the leek, use a small, sliced courgette; degorge and squeeze it dry as described on page 74 before cooking.

Red Pepper Timbale

½ red pepper, sliced
1 small shallot, finely chopped
1 egg, beaten

40g/1½oz Ricotta cheese, sieved
paprika, salt and lemon juice, to taste

Cook the pepper and shallot in a little water until very soft. Increase the heat to drive off excess moisture then purée with the egg and cheese. Add paprika, salt and lemon juice to taste. Transfer to a 10cm/4in ramekin dish, cover with a dome of greaseproof paper, place in a steaming basket, colander or large sieve placed over boiling water in a pan, cover and steam for about 7 minutes or until lightly set.

Sweetcorn Drop Scones

To make the drop scones without a blender, put the flour and seasoning into a bowl, break in the egg and gradually stir in the milk to make a smooth batter. Chop the sweetcorn before adding.

The drop scones can be served as a first course, a snack, supper or light lunch dish, as a vegetable accompaniment, or with bacon, sautéed mushrooms, or eggs.

If you do not want to eat all six at once, any leftover cooked scones can be kept, covered, in a cool place then fried briefly on both sides to reheat. Alternatively, keep some uncooked batter covered in the refrigerator and use to make sweetcorn 'popovers' (don't expect them to rise in quite the same way as normal popovers, but they should still be light) – pour a little oil into 3 approximately 5cm/2in patty tins and put them into the oven while heating it to 200°C/400°F/gas mark 6. When the oven is hot, divide the sweetcorn batter between the patty tins and cook for about 12–15 minutes – this should leave the centres still slightly moist. These are particularly good if flavoured with cheese – about 15g/½oz for half the basic mixture.

55g/2oz plain flour	55g/2oz cooked fresh, or
salt and freshly ground black	thawed frozen, or well-
pepper	drained canned sweetcorn
1 small egg	kernels
5 tablespoons milk	oil, for cooking

Mix the flour, seasoning, egg and milk together in a blender until smooth, then add the sweetcorn and mix briefly to break the kernels up slightly, leaving a nubbly texture.

Heat a very little oil in a heavy nonstick frying pan then drop in tablespoonfuls of the batter, spacing them well apart. Cook until lightly browned underneath then turn them over and cook on the other side. Transfer to kitchen paper to drain then keep warm in a folded tea towel.

VARIATIONS

- Flavour the batter with chopped shallot that has been slowly fried until soft and golden brown, and some finely grated, well-flavoured Cheddar or Parmesan cheese.
- Add a generous teaspoon of finely chopped fresh chives or parsley, or slightly less tarragon, to the prepared mixture.
- Blend about 30g/1oz chopped well-flavoured cheese with the batter; if making it by hand, grate the cheese finely.
- Suggested toppings – Chicken Livers on Soured Cream or Yogurt – lightly cook approximately 85g/3oz chopped chicken

livers, add a couple of dashes of dry sherry, Madeira or red wine, bubble briefly to reduce then add seasoning and mustard to taste. Spread the scones with chilled soured cream or Greek yogurt and top with the chicken liver mixture.

– sauté a rasher of bacon with about 30g/1oz diced mushrooms then add a small diced tomato, and flavour with chopped chives or parsley. Divide between the scones.

Bacon Fraise

The origins of this dish, a cross between a light pancake and an omelette with a layer of savoury filling running through the centre, go back as far as the fifteenth century, when it was probably cooked in hot fat collected in a dish placed beneath a spit-roasted joint.

Serve with sautéed mushrooms and grilled or raw tomatoes, or a salad.

30g/1oz 4 level tablespoons plain flour
1 small egg and 1 small egg white
5 tablespoons milk

freshly ground black pepper
2 rashers bacon, cut into strips
unsalted butter, oil or bacon fat (optional)

Sift the flour into a bowl, make a well in the centre and drop in the whole egg. Gradually add the milk, beating well to make a smooth batter. Season with black pepper.

Gently cook the bacon in a nonstick frying pan until the fat runs and the bacon is crisp. Using a slotted spoon, transfer to absorbent paper to drain. Whisk the egg white until stiff but not dry then lightly fold into the batter. If necessary, add a little butter, oil or bacon fat to the bacon fat in the pan and heat until it begins to sizzle. Pour in half of the batter, spreading it out to cover the base of the pan. Cook over a moderate heat until the bottom is lightly browned and the top just set. Scatter the bacon over the surface then cover with the remaining batter. Cook until the top is set then turn the 'cake' over and cook until brown underneath.

VARIATIONS

- Cook any of the following vegetables with the bacon – chopped onion or shallot, leeks, mushrooms, courgettes. Other vegetables, such as sweetcorn or peas, can be stirred into the bacon just before it is ready and heated through while the bacon continues cooking.
- Flavour the batter with herbs, such as chives, or with horseradish sauce, mustard, Tabasco sauce or Worcestershire sauce.
- Cheese and Onion Fraise – as a filling use 1 fried chopped onion and a generous sprinkling of grated full-flavoured cheese or diced softer cheese, such as Brie or a soft goat's cheese.
- Ham and Cheese Fraise – fill with chopped ham and cheese.

Ricotta Tarts

Ricotta cheese has a low fat content, but if an egg yolk is added it tastes deceptively rich and is beautifully smooth; if the egg white is included too the filling will be lighter in both texture and taste.

If there is too much filling for the bread case you are using, the excess can be cooked in a small ramekin dish until just set, or spooned into seasoned mushroom caps and baked – 5cm/2in mushrooms require about 6 minutes.

approximately 150g/5oz
  Ricotta cheese
2 egg yolks or 1 egg, beaten
large pinch finely chopped
  fresh chives

salt and freshly ground black
  pepper
2 7.5cm/3in bread cases (see
  page 21)

Beat the Ricotta until smooth then stir in the egg, chives and
seasoning. Spoon into the bread cases and bake at 180°C/350°F/
gas mark 4 for about 12–15 minutes or until lightly set in the
centre. Eat warm or cold.

VARIATIONS
- Add a little sautéed, finely chopped shallot.
- Omit the chives; gently spread a little pesto over the top of the
  cooked tarts and return to the oven for about 5 minutes.

PASTAS, PIZZAS AND RICE

Pasta

It is so easy to make pasta tasty and different. Instant flavourings include sauces or pastes, such as mayonnaise, Aïoli (see page 239), anchovy or olive paste, Tapenade (see page 240), Anchoïaide (see page 241), pesto, diluted perhaps with cream or Greek yogurt, or some of the Chinese sauces – try hoisin or yellow bean paste – herbs, seeds, or simply different oils – olive, walnut, sesame.

Most of the following recipes do not specify any particular type of pasta as it does not really matter which is used. The amount of pasta, too, depends on individual tastes and appetites, and the weight specified is only a guideline.

Pasta with Potted Shrimps or Prawns

Potted shrimps and prawns are quite widely available. Have the shrimps or prawns at room temperature, cook some pasta then drain it and return it to the saucepan over a low heat. Toss with the shrimps or prawns and their butter and finish with grated Parmesan and plenty of freshly ground black pepper. Some lightly cooked chopped mushrooms or red peppers are a good addition.

Pasta with Black Olive and Walnut Paste

approximately 85–115g/
  3–4oz pasta
a small spoonful or so of Black
  Olive and Walnut Paste (see
  page 242)

1½–2 tablespoons cream or
  Greek yogurt
diced red pepper (roasted and
  peeled, if liked)

Cook the pasta in plenty of boiling water until only just tender. Drain well, return to the saucepan over a low heat and toss with the black olive and walnut paste, cream or Greek yogurt, and red pepper.

Pasta with Prawns and Tomatoes

approximately 85g/3oz pasta
olive oil
1 shallot, finely chopped
1 small clove garlic, crushed
1–2 tomatoes, skinned, seeded
  and chopped
55g/2oz cooked peeled prawns

small pinch cayenne pepper
salt and freshly ground black
  pepper
chopped fresh parsley
freshly grated Parmesan
  cheese (optional)

Cook the pasta in plenty of boiling salted water until only just tender. Meanwhile, heat a little oil in a heavy nonstick pan. Add the shallot and garlic and cook, stirring occasionally, for 2–3 minutes. Add the tomatoes and cook until lightly thickened. Add the prawns and heat through. Add cayenne pepper, salt and freshly ground black pepper to taste.

Drain the pasta well. Tip into a warmed serving bowl, add the sauce, a little chopped parsley and some grated Parmesan cheese, if using, and toss together.

VARIATION
- Add some diced red pepper to the tomato mixture.

——————— *Pasta with Spinach and Ricotta* ———————

approximately 85g/3oz pasta
small knob unsalted butter
anchovy paste
55g/2oz frozen leaf spinach,
   thawed, well-drained and
   chopped

approximately 40g/1½oz
   Ricotta cheese
approximately 1–2
   tablespoons freshly grated
   Parmesan cheese
salt and freshly ground black
   pepper

Cook the pasta in plenty of boiling salted water until just tender. Meanwhile, melt a small knob of butter in a small saucepan. Stir in anchovy paste to taste then add the spinach and heat through completely.

Drain the pasta well, transfer to a serving bowl, add the spinach, Ricotta, a little extra butter, if liked, and the Parmesan cheese. Toss together and add salt and black pepper.

VARIATION
- Blend the Ricotta with a spoonful or two of cream or Greek yogurt and heat through gently before tossing with the pasta.
- Instead of using anchovy paste, grate a little nutmeg over the spinach and season with salt.

——— *Pasta with Courgettes and Tarragon* ———

approximately 115g/4oz small
   courgettes, cut into thin
   matchsticks
salt
approximately 85g/3oz pasta
unsalted butter
½–1 teaspoon finely chopped

fresh tarragon, or small
   pinch dried tarragon
2 tablespoons cream or Greek
   yogurt
freshly grated Parmesan
   cheese

Put the courgettes into a colander, sprinkle salt over and leave for about 30–60 minutes. Rinse, drain well, and dry on absorbent paper.

Cook the pasta in plenty of boiling salted water until just tender.

Meanwhile, heat a small knob of butter, add the courgettes and cook over a fairly high heat, stirring frequently, until a light golden brown. Stir in the tarragon and cream or yogurt. If using cream, bubble briefly until lightly thickened. If using yogurt, just allow it to heat through. Season to taste.

Drain the pasta and tip into a warmed serving bowl. Add a little more butter, if liked, and about 1–2 tablespoons Parmesan cheese; toss briefly then add the courgettes. Toss together and sprinkle extra Parmesan over.

—— *Pasta with Peppers and Mushrooms* ——

approximately 85g/3oz pasta
small knob unsalted butter
1 small shallot, finely chopped
1 small clove garlic, finely
   crushed
1 tablespoon medium-bodied
   dry white wine (optional)
approximately 85g/3oz
   mushrooms, preferably
   oyster, shiitake, or brown
   cap (chestnut), thickly sliced

½ red pepper, preferably
   roasted and skinned (see
   page 50), thinly sliced
1–2 tablespoons double cream
   or Greek yogurt
approximately ½ teaspoon
   finely chopped fresh
   tarragon, or pinch dried
   tarragon
salt and freshly ground black
   pepper

Cook the pasta in plenty of boiling salted water until just tender.

Meanwhile, melt the butter, add the shallot and garlic and cook over a moderate heat until softened but not coloured. Add the wine, if using, and boil until reduced by half. Add the mushrooms and cook, stirring occasionally, for 3–5 minutes. Add the red pepper and cream or yogurt. If using cream, bubble for a minute or two until lightly thickened. Add tarragon and seasoning to taste.

Drain the pasta thoroughly and turn into a warmed serving bowl. Add the sauce and toss well.

—————— *Pasta with Seeds* ——————

Fusilli is a good shape for this dish as the spirals trap the seeds. Change the character of the recipe by using different oils – a mild or a fruity olive oil, or a proportion of walnut, hazelnut or sesame oil. Use just sunflower or sesame seeds, or a mixture of the two.

approximately 85g/3oz fusilli   oil
2–3 teaspoons sunflower seeds   freshly ground black pepper
2–3 teaspoons sesame seeds

Cook the pasta in boiling salted water until just tender.

Meanwhile, heat some sunflower and sesame seeds in a heavy nonstick, pan until brown, but not burnt.

Drain the pasta well and quickly return to the pan. Add a little oil to the seeds, then toss well with the pasta. Add freshly ground black pepper and serve.

VARIATIONS
- Add a little finely chopped garlic with the oil.
- For an oriental flavour omit the oil and toss the pasta with a sauce made from 1 tablespoon hoisin sauce, ½ teaspoon light soy sauce, 1 teaspoon chilli bean sauce.

_____ Pasta with Onion, Mushrooms _____
and Feta

approximately 55g/2oz
   tagliatelle
olive oil
1 small onion, sliced into rings
55g/2oz mushrooms,
   quartered or chopped
1 teaspoon fresh oregano or ½
   teaspoon dried oregano
1–2 tablespoons cream,

fromage blanc, soft cheese
   or Greek yogurt
dash lemon juice
freshly ground black pepper
walnut oil (optional)
approximately 30g/1oz Feta
   cheese
chopped fresh parsley

Cook the pasta in plenty of boiling salted water until just tender. Meanwhile heat a little olive oil in a small pan over a moderate heat, add the onion and cook gently for 10 minutes. Add the mushrooms and oregano, and cook for 5 minutes. Stir in the cream, fromage blanc, cheese or yogurt – if using cream, bubble until thickened slightly. Sprinkle over a little lemon juice and plenty of black pepper.

Drain the pasta well, toss immediately with a little walnut oil, if using, or olive oil then with the mushrooms and onion mixture. Crumble the Feta cheese over, and sprinkle with parsley.

VARIATION
- If oregano is not available, use tarragon, chives, marjoram or thyme.

Pasta with Soft Cheese, Bacon and Mushrooms

approximately 85g/3oz pasta
small knob unsalted butter
40g/1½oz bacon, chopped
40g/1½oz mushrooms, sliced
approximately 40g/1½oz
    herb-flavoured soft cheese

1 tablespoon single cream,
    fromage blanc or Greek
    yogurt (optional)
freshly ground black pepper
freshly grated Parmesan, to
    serve

Cook the pasta in plenty of boiling salted water until just tender.

Meanwhile melt a very small amount of butter in a saucepan, add the bacon and cook over a moderate heat for 2–3 minutes. Stir in the mushrooms and cook for a further 2–3 minutes or so.

Drain the pasta well, quickly return to the saucepan, toss in the bacon and mushroom mixture, the cheese, and cream, fromage blanc or yogurt, if using. Toss briefly and season with black pepper. Serve with freshly grated Parmesan sprinkled over.

VARIATIONS
- Other vegetables can be used with or instead of the mush-rooms e.g. onion or shallot, red pepper, peas, sweetcorn,

courgette, diced green beans or broccoli. Cook them or heat them through as necessary.

• Substitute diced ham for bacon, adding it with the soft cheese.

———— Pasta with Parsley and Nut Sauce ————

30g/1oz walnuts or almonds
15g/½oz parsley sprigs
1½ tablespoons freshly grated
  Parmesan cheese, plus extra
  to serve
4 tablespoons olive oil

30g/1oz soft, mild goat's
  cheese, or other soft cheese
salt and freshly ground black
  pepper
approximately 85g/3oz pasta

Process the nuts and parsley in a blender until fairly finely chopped. With the machine still on, blend in the Parmesan then add the oil, a drop at a time. Stir in the goat's cheese and adjust the seasoning to taste.

Cook the pasta in plenty of boiling salted water until just tender. Meanwhile, heat the sauce gently but do not allow to boil. Drain the pasta well, tip immediately on to a warmed plate, pour the sauce over and toss to mix. Serve with extra Parmesan.

Pizzas

It is not essential to make your own pizza base as it is now possible to buy partly baked ones sealed in packets, which can be kept at room temperature until opened.

The toppings below will cover one pizza about 19cm/7½in in diameter. If necessary, adjust the quantities to fit your pizza base.

The toppings can also be served on large slices of toast or French bread.

Pizza with Goat's Cheese, Onion and Olives

2 tablespoons olive oil
1 onion, sliced
1 clove garlic, crushed
salt and freshly ground black
    pepper
55g/2oz Mozzarella cheese,
    grated
115g/4oz creamy goat's cheese

8 black olives, stoned and
    halved
2 tomatoes, skinned, seeded
    and chopped, and 1 tomato,
    skinned and sliced
fresh herbs – mostly parsley
    and thyme with some
    rosemary – finely chopped

Heat half of the oil in a frying pan, add the onion and garlic and cook until the onion is soft and transparent. Season to taste.

Brush the pizza base with the remaining oil then cover with the onion and garlic. Scatter the Mozzarella evenly over the top then scatter the goat's cheese, olives and chopped tomatoes over. Arrange the sliced tomato on top. Bake at 220°C/425°F/gas mark 7 for 20–25 minutes or until the pizza base has risen and the cheese has melted. Remove from the oven and sprinkle with the herbs.

VARIATIONS
● Substitute 2 sun-dried tomatoes cut into fine strips, for the fresh tomatoes.
● Add some capers and a chopped anchovy fillet.

—————— *Tomato and Pesto Pizza* ——————

olive oil
salt and freshly ground black
   pepper
3 medium tomatoes, sliced
approximately 3 tablespoons
   pesto
1 clove garlic, finely crushed

½ small onion, preferably a
   red one, thinly sliced
55g/2oz Mozzarella cheese,
   thinly sliced
6 black olives, stoned and
   sliced

Sprinkle a little oil and some salt and black pepper over the tomatoes. Spread the pesto over the pizza base. Scatter the garlic and onion over the pesto, followed by the tomatoes then lay overlapping slices of cheese over the entire surface. Bake at 220°C/425°F/gas mark 7 for 20–25 minutes or until the cheese has melted and the base has risen. Scatter the olives over.

——————— *Onion, Blue Cheese and* ———————
Walnut Pizza

200g/7oz onions
15g/½oz unsalted butter
1½ teaspoons olive oil
30g/1oz walnuts, chopped

1½ teaspoons finely chopped
   fresh thyme
55g/2oz blue Brie, finely
   chopped
freshly ground black pepper

Cut the onions in half then slice thinly. Heat the butter and oil, add the onions and cook gently for 4–5 minutes, stirring at intervals, until the onions are soft and lightly coloured. Leave to cool slightly then spread evenly over the pizza base, taking them right up to the edge. Scatter the nuts, thyme and cheese evenly over the onions. Grind black pepper over then bake at 200°C/

425°F/gas mark 7 for 20–25 minutes or until the cheese has melted and the base has risen well.

———— *Red Pepper and Olive Pizza* ————

55g/2oz stoned black olives
1 tablespoon olive oil
1 small clove garlic, peeled
1 small shallot, chopped
2 small–medium red peppers, roasted, halved, deseeded

and chopped
85g/3oz Emmenthal or Gruyère, coarsely grated
finely chopped fresh parsley and shallot, for garnish

Reserve 3 of the olives and slice them. Process the remainder with the oil, garlic and shallot in a blender until smooth. Spread evenly over the pizza surface then scatter the red peppers evenly over the sauce, sprinkle with the cheese then the reserved olives.

Bake at 220°C/425°F/gas mark 7 for 20–25 minutes or until the cheese has melted and the pizza base has risen.

Sprinkle with mixed parsley and shallot and serve hot.

Rice

Rice is a good vehicle for other ingredients, and is very easy to flavour either during the cooking or afterwards. In fact, when I am cooking rice I invariably add something to complement the flavours in the dish it is to accompany. This may be as simple as adding herbs to the cooking water, such as a bay leaf, fennel or dill (the leaves or seeds). Parsley is good if the rice is to be served with fish, particularly if some lemon juice and a little grated rind are stirred into the rice after cooking, and rosemary goes well with lamb. You could also fry some spice seeds (coriander, cardamom, cumin) or a generous sprinkling of paprika in butter or oil then add the rice and stir for a couple of minutes before pouring in the liquid and cooking as normal.

Herbs or different types of oils can be mixed in with unflavoured boiled rice; unsalted butter and finely grated Parmesan is another quick way of adding flavour, and for a contrasting 'crunch' try seeds, such as sesame or sunflower, or chopped nuts. Simple flavourings that can be stirred into hot or cold rice include oyster or anchovy sauce, mustard, pesto, Anchoïaide (see page 241), Tapenade (see page 240), green olive paste, or flavoured butter (see page 244). For creamy rice, stir through fromage blanc, soft, medium-fat or full-fat cheese, mayonnaise or Aïoli (see page 239).

Small amounts of chopped, cooked vegetables can be added to the rice if it is to be served as an accompaniment; if it is to be served as a main dish, cooked fish or meats, plus other flavourings, can be added.

Rice Salads

If making a salad using cold leftover rice, and if time allows, warm the dressing, stir in the rice to coat then leave to cool again. If cooking rice especially for a salad, stir the dressing into the freshly cooked rice and leave to cool.

You can then add fresh vegetables or store-cupboard ingredients such as nuts – lightly toasted are best – herbs, olives, capers, canned tuna, smoked mussels, sardines, salmon, crab, anchovy fillets, diced cheese, bacon, dried fruits, cooked chicken or turkey.

Fried Vegetables and Rice with Oyster Sauce

The vegetables can be varied by the inclusion of, for example, mangetout, or ordinary peas, leeks, spring onions, courgettes or red peppers.

55g/2oz long grain rice
1½ teaspoons olive oil
55g/2oz carrots, finely
   chopped

55g/2oz French beans, chopped
approximately 1–1½
   teaspoons oyster sauce
freshly ground black pepper

Cook the rice in boiling salted water until tender then drain well.

Heat half of the oil to a high temperature and stir-fry the carrots and French beans for about a minute. Using a slotted spoon, transfer to absorbent paper to drain.

Heat the remaining oil to a high temperature in the same pan. Add the rice and stir-fry for 1 minute. Stir in the oyster sauce, carrots and beans and cook for 2 minutes, stirring. Season with black pepper.

——— Ham and Parmesan Risotto ———

This recipe is for a genuine Italian risotto, which can only be made with Italian medium-grain arborio rice. Important points to remember when making risotto are to use *boiling* stock, or water; to add the liquid a little at a time, making sure it is completely absorbed before the next addition; to stir constantly; and to adjust the amount of liquid so the final result holds together with a creamy but not sticky texture, and the grains of rice are just tender.

approximately 300ml/½ pint
   chicken, veal or vegetable
   stock
unsalted butter
olive oil
1 small shallot, finely chopped
15g/½oz prosciutto crudo
   (raw ham), chopped

85g/3oz arborio rice
salt and freshly ground black
   pepper
freshly grated Parmesan
   cheese
chopped fresh parsley
   (optional)

In a small pan, heat the stock and keep it at simmering point while you make the risotto. Heat a little butter and olive oil in a heavy pan, add the shallot and prosciutto and cook over a moderate heat, stirring occasionally, until the shallot has softened and become a very light, golden brown. Stir in the rice, continue to stir for 2 minutes then add a tablespoonful of the stock. When the stock has been absorbed by the rice, add another spoonful. Cook, stirring, until this, too, has been absorbed. Continue adding stock, stirring constantly and cooking in the same way until the rice is just cooked and the risotto creamy – about 20 minutes. Season. You may not need all the stock. Remove the pan from the heat, put a small knob of butter and a tablespoon or so of grated Parmesan on top, cover and leave for a minute until the butter has melted. Stir well, sprinkle parsley over, if liked, and serve immediately.

VARIATIONS

- Mushroom Risotto (1) – add approximately 85g/3oz lightly sautéed brown cap (chestnut) mushrooms about 5 minutes before the end of the cooking. Omit the Parmesan cheese.
- Mushroom Risotto (2) – if you cannot buy brown cap (chestnut) mushrooms, use approximately 55g/2oz button mushrooms plus approximately 7g/¼oz dried ones; these should be soaked in a little hot water for about 20 minutes, then chopped and added with the prosciutto. Use the soaking liquor (brought to the boil) instead of the first spoonful of stock. Omit the Parmesan cheese.
- Asparagus Broccoli or Courgette Risotto – use a little more cheese, and stir in with it approximately 85–115g/3–4oz lightly cooked asparagus tips, broccoli florets or sliced steamed courgettes; use chervil, if available, instead of parsley with the asparagus, and tarragon, marjoram or thyme with the courgettes.

VEGETABLES

Many people cooking for one find fresh vegetables inconvenient to prepare. An avocado or a cauliflower, for example, is usually too large for one meal so you have to either eat the same thing on successive days, or find the shrivelled or mouldy remains days later in the vegetable rack. Even if you freeze the remaining portion you end up with a freezer full of small packages of vegetables, most of which will not be at their best.

There is a number of ways, though, of using up surplus vegetables – chopped, sliced or cut into strips for stir-fry dishes; tossed with rice and pasta; filling omelettes; made into salads or soups; or puréed for serving as an accompaniment or as a base for scrambled or poached eggs.

Most of the recipes in this section are multi-functional – sometimes I make them for a first course, sometimes a snack or light meal, other times as a vegetable accompaniment.

Vegetable Purées

Purées can be made from leftover cooked vegetables but they are better if made from freshly cooked ones; it is best to steam the vegetables as it keeps them drier.

Cook the vegetables, drain, then mash or blend to a purée. Heat the purée in a thick-bottomed pan over a moderately low heat, stirring with a wooden spoon, until surplus moisture has been driven off, then beat in fromage frais, Greek yogurt, soft cheese, cream, butter, or an egg yolk. Use cheese, herbs or spices to flavour the purée (for ideas on combinations see Soups, page 14).

Purées can also be made into croquettes, coated in ground or finely chopped nuts, breadcrumbs, oats or sesame seeds, and fried in fairly hot oil until crisp and golden on the outside – if the oil is not hot enough the croquette will become soggy.

Broccoli with Lemon and Sesame Seeds

approximately 115g/4oz broccoli florets

a little unsalted butter

approximately 2 teaspoons lemon juice

1–2 teaspoons lightly toasted sesame seeds

salt and freshly ground black pepper

Steam the broccoli florets until tender. Meanwhile melt the butter in a small pan, add the lemon juice, sesame seeds and seasoning. When the broccoli is cooked, add to the pan and toss lightly together.

VARIATION
● Try this recipe using cauliflower, carrots, leeks, parsnips, celeriac or Jerusalem artichokes.

Stuffed Cabbage Leaves

3 tablespoons chicken, veal or
  vegetable stock (optional)
1 dried mushroom (cep or
  porcini), chopped
2 cabbage leaves
55g/2oz mushrooms, finely
  chopped
½ small red pepper, blanched
  in boiling water for 1
  minute, drained, rinsed and
  chopped
1 tablespoon chopped fresh
  chives
30g/1oz Ricotta cheese, sieved
1 small egg, separated
salt and freshly ground black
  pepper
2 juniper berries, crushed
2 small sprigs thyme or
  tarragon

Bring the stock or an equivalent amount of water to the boil, pour it over the cep or porcini and leave to soak for 20–30 minutes.

Meanwhile, cut the central rib from the cabbage leaves. Drape the leaves over the back of a sieve and pour boiling water over them to soften them. Dry on absorbent paper.

Strain the dried mushroom, reserving the liquor. Mix the fresh mushrooms with the dried mushroom, red pepper and chives then the Ricotta. Beat the egg yolk then mix it into the mushroom mixture and season to taste.

Whisk the egg white until stiff but not dry then fold gently into the mushroom mixture. Divide between the cabbage leaves, then fold them over to make neat parcels.

Place the parcels seam-side down in a buttered small heatproof dish that they just fit. Scatter the juniper berries over and lay a herb sprig on each parcel. Strain the reserved mushroom liquor over the parcels. Put the dish in a steamer or colander, place over a saucepan of boiling water, cover tightly and steam for about 35 minutes until the filling is lightly set. Serve with the cooking juices spooned over.

VARIATION
- Substitute lettuce or chard leaves for the cabbage leaves.

Stuffed Vegetables

Many recipes for stuffed vegetables include breadcrumbs, rice or some other starchy ingredient, which I have always thought to be wrong as it makes the mixture too heavy for the containing vegetable. Here are a couple of recipes for creamy fillings that complement and contrast with, in the first case, cool, moist tomatoes, in the second, crisp mushrooms. Serve as snacks, or for a first course.

Stuffed Tomatoes

Black Olive and Walnut Paste (see page 242)

Greek yogurt or fromage blanc tomatoes

Blend a little of the black olive and walnut paste with just over half the amount of yogurt or fromage blanc.

Cut the tomatoes in half, or remove a slice from the top. Scoop out the flesh and add to the paste mixture. Mix together well then spoon into the tomato halves.

Stuffed Mushrooms

Either use a flavoured soft cheese, or add flavourings of your own, such as mustard, anchovy paste, horseradish or chopped herbs, to plain cheese.

lemon juice

brown or white button
   mushrooms, stalks removed

salt and freshly ground black
   pepper

soft cheese – plain, or
   flavoured with herbs, garlic
   etc.

Sprinkle lemon juice over the mushrooms and season inside the caps. Place them gill-side uppermost. Grill, if preferred, or leave raw. Season the cheese, if necessary, and spoon into the caps.

Peperonata

Peperonata is an Italian version of ratatouille, made with red peppers, onions, tomatoes and garlic. It can be used and stored in the same way as Ratatouille (see below).

olive oil

1 small–medium onion, thinly
   sliced

1 clove garlic, sliced

2 medium red peppers, sliced

225g/½lb ripe tomatoes,
   peeled and chopped

salt and freshly ground black
   pepper

chopped fresh parsley or basil

Heat the oil in a heavy nonstick pan, add the onion and cook, stirring occasionally, until softened. Add the garlic and red peppers then the tomatoes. Stir everything together well, bring to a simmer, lower the heat and cook, uncovered, stirring occasionally, for about 25 minutes, or until the peppers are soft and almost all the surplus liquid has evaporated. Season to taste and serve with chopped parsley or basil scattered over.

Ratatouille

Ratatouille is an extremely useful dish as it can be served as an accompaniment to meats or simply cooked fish, made into a bed for poached eggs, used as a filling for omelettes or frittatas, spooned on to rice, or on to toast, toasted rolls or baguettes, served with cheese scattered over and grilled, or thinned down slightly to make a tasty sauce for pasta.

The proportions of the vegetables can be varied, and so can how they are prepared – whether sliced or chopped – and the way they are cooked. Some versions involve frying the vegetables separately, which is rather time-consuming; in others, all the vegetables are cooked together all the time. However, I prefer the method below, which is a compromise between the two and leaves the vegetables soft but still intact in a thick, tomatoey sauce.

I prefer to make ratatouille in advance and always cook enough for more than one meal, because the flavours improve on standing, it reheats beautifully, and it can be used in so many ways. The quantity below makes 2 servings.

225g/½lb aubergines, sliced
olive oil
175g/6oz onions, half
   chopped, half thinly sliced
2 cloves garlic, crushed
225g/½lb well-flavoured
   tomatoes, peeled, seeded
   and chopped

225g/½lb red peppers, sliced
225g/½lb courgettes, half
   chopped, half sliced
salt and freshly ground black
   pepper
chopped fresh herbs e.g. basil,
   parsley, thyme, marjoram,
   tarragon, chives (optional)

If preferred, put the aubergine into a colander, sprinkle salt over and leave to drain for 30–60 minutes. Rinse, drain well and pat dry.

Heat some oil in a heavy nonstick pan – the amount depends on how much oil you like in your cooking. Add the onions and garlic and cook, stirring occasionally, until softened but not coloured. Stir in the tomatoes and cook over a reasonably brisk heat for about 5 minutes. Add the peppers and aubergines, stir well and cook gently for about 15 minutes. Stir in the courgettes and continue to cook gently, uncovered, for about 45–60 minutes. If there is a lot of liquor, spoon it off into another pan and boil until well reduced. Pour it back into the vegetables, season, and add some herbs, if you like.

Aubergine Slices with Pizza Topping

I first cooked aubergine slices in this way when I had part of an aubergine left. I enjoyed it so much, I now make it as a planned dish. The aubergine slices can be cut either across or lengthways.

aubergine slices, about 0.5 cm/ ¼in thick	Mozzarella cheese
salt	tomato, skinned, seeds removed, finely chopped
olive oil	freshly ground black pepper

Sprinkle the aubergine slices with salt and leave in a colander to drain for about an hour.

Dry the aubergine with absorbent kitchen paper then lightly brush both sides of each slice with olive oil. Lay the slices on a grill rack lined with foil, or on a baking sheet. Place under a preheated grill for about 3 minutes per side until golden. Cover the aubergine with slices of Mozzarella, top with chopped tomato and olive oil, sprinkle generously with black pepper then place under the grill again until the cheese has melted.

VARIATION
- Add a small pinch of fresh herbs to the tomatoes – e.g. basil or oregano.

Stuffed Aubergine Slices

1 aubergine, cut into 1cm/⅓in
   slices
salt
1 tablespoon olive oil
1 small clove garlic, finely
   crushed
freshly ground black pepper
approximately 40g/1½oz tuna
   in brine, drained

½ anchovy fillet, or anchovy
   purée to taste
approximately 2 teaspoons
   mayonnaise
2 teaspoons chopped capers
Tabasco sauce
lemon juice

Sprinkle the aubergine slices with salt and leave in a colander to drain for about an hour. Dry with absorbent kitchen paper.

Put the oil into a small bowl and mix in the garlic and plenty of black pepper. Brush the aubergine slices with the oil and place under a preheated grill for about 3 minutes or until golden. Watch to make sure they do not brown too quickly, and if necessary reduce the heat.

Mash the tuna and anchovy together until evenly blended then mix in sufficient mayonnaise to give the consistency of a thick mousse. Add the capers, Tabasco sauce, lemon juice and black pepper to taste. Spread over each aubergine slice and roll up quite firmly like a Swiss roll.

Place with the join underneath. Eat warm or cold.

Aubergine with Mint

This dish is very good eaten warm but it tastes even better if the flavours are allowed to mature overnight. Use a good oil and flavourful tomatoes.

1 small aubergine, sliced
1 teaspoon lemon juice
1 small clove garlic
1 teaspoon chopped fresh mint
1 tablespoon olive oil

4 large black olives, stoned
   and chopped
salt and freshly ground black
   pepper
1 tomato, peeled and chopped

Put the aubergine into a smallish pan with the lemon juice and 5 tablespoons water. Bring just to the boil then cover and simmer gently for 10 minutes or until the liquid has been absorbed and the aubergine becomes translucent. Chop the slices into quarters. Chop the garlic and mint together then stir into the aubergine with the oil, olives, black pepper and just a little salt, until evenly mixed. Leave to cool then add the tomato. Serve cold.

—————— *Broad Beans with Bacon* ——————

1 green (unsmoked) back
   bacon rasher, cut into strips
1 shallot, finely chopped
85–115g/3–4oz fresh broad
   beans (shelled weight), or
   frozen ones, thawed, or
   canned ones, drained and
   rinsed

2–3 tablespoons chicken, veal
   or vegetable stock (optional)
1–2 tablespoons single cream,
   Greek yogurt or fromage
   blanc (optional)
salt and freshly ground black
   pepper
crisp croutons, to serve
   (optional)

Cook the bacon in a small, heavy frying pan until the fat begins to run, add the shallot and continue to cook over a fairly low heat until the shallot begins to soften. Add the broad beans and the stock, if using, or an equivalent amount of water plus salt. Bring to the boil, cover and cook until the beans are just tender, or until warmed through completely if using thawed frozen ones or canned ones. Add a little more liquid if necessary. Stir in the cream, yogurt or fromage blanc, if using, and season to taste.

Serve with croutons sprinkled over, if liked – garlic-flavoured ones are particularly good.

VARIATIONS
- Broad Beans with Parma Ham – omit the bacon and cook the shallot in about 2 teaspoons olive oil. A couple of minutes before the beans are ready, stir in about 30g/1oz Parma ham, cut into strips.
- Substitute peas for broad beans in either of the above recipes.

Brussels Sprouts with Sesame Seeds

115g/4oz Brussels sprouts, trimmed

approximately 2–3 teaspoons freshly grated Parmesan cheese

approximately 1 teaspoon sesame seeds

freshly ground black pepper

4 tablespoons Greek yogurt, or double or soured cream

salt

Steam the sprouts until they are just tender then tip into a flameproof dish. Meanwhile, mix together the Parmesan, sesame seeds and black pepper, and season the yogurt or cream with a little salt. Spoon the yogurt or cream over the sprouts, sprinkle with the cheese mixture and place under a preheated grill until bubbling.

VARIATION
- Instead of grilling, simply tip the steamed sprouts into a saucepan, add the yogurt or cream, cheese and seasoning and heat through, stirring. Serve with toasted sesame seeds sprinkled over the top.

Cauliflower with Fluffy Cheese Sauce

The savoury, light sauce goes equally well with Brussels sprouts and broccoli.

175g/6oz cauliflower florets
5 tablespoons thick
  mayonnaise
2 small eggs, separated
30g/1oz mature Cheddar
  cheese, grated

approximately 1 teaspoon
  Dijon mustard
approximately ½–1 teaspoon
  finely grated lemon rind
freshly ground black pepper
freshly grated Parmesan
  cheese

Steam the cauliflower florets so that they retain their crispness, then put into a buttered, shallow ovenproof dish. Mix together the mayonnaise, egg yolks and Cheddar cheese with mustard, lemon rind and black pepper to taste. Whisk the egg whites until stiff but not dry then fold lightly into the cheese mixture until just evenly blended. Carefully spoon over the cauliflower so that it is completely covered, sprinkle a little Parmesan over the top and place in an oven preheated to 190°C/375°F/gas mark 5, or a little distance away from a preheated moderate grill, until risen and golden.

Smoked Oyster- or Mussel-stuffed Courgette

1 medium courgette, cut in half lengthways
55g/2oz smoked oysters or mussels, each one cut in half
15g/½oz unsalted butter
2 tablespoons double cream, crème fraîche, fromage blanc or Greek yogurt
1 egg yolk
1 teaspoon dry sherry
freshly ground black pepper
lemon juice (optional)
parsley, for garnish

Steam the courgette over boiling salted water for about 5–6 minutes. Remove from the heat and leave until cool enough to handle then cut in half lengthways and scoop out the seeds.

Heat the oysters or mussels in the butter in a small pan. Mix the cream, crème fraîche, fromage blanc or yogurt into the egg yolk then stir into the pan and cook slowly, stirring gently, until thickened. Do not allow the mixture to boil.

Remove from the heat, stir in the sherry and season with black pepper and a little lemon juice, if necessary.

Spoon into the courgette halves. Leave to cool then chill in the fridge before serving, garnished with parsley.

Cheese-stuffed Courgette

A tomato sauce goes well with these courgette boats.

1 large courgette, about 150–175g/5–6oz, halved lengthways
30g/1oz soft goat's cheese, or flavoured soft cheese
2–3 teaspoons fine fresh breadcrumbs
salt and freshly ground black pepper
1 small egg white

Steam the courgette halves over boiling salted water for about 6 minutes or until tender.

Remove from the heat and leave cut-side down on absorbent kitchen paper to drain and cool. When cool enough to handle, scoop out the centres with a teaspoon. Purée the flesh then mix with the cheese, breadcrumbs and seasoning.

Whisk the egg white until stiff but not dry then lightly fold into the cheese mixture until just evenly blended.

Place the courgette halves, hollowed-out-side uppermost, on a baking sheet. Stuff with the cheese mixture then place them a little distance below a hot grill for about 7 minutes until the filling is set and a light golden brown.

VARIATION

● Feta Cheese-stuffed Courgette – steam the courgette and remove the flesh as above, then beat the flesh with 30g/1oz crumbled Feta cheese, 1 small egg, a pinch of chopped fresh parsley and seasoning. Grill as above.

─────── *Savoury Cabbage* ───────

A flavourful accompaniment to sausages, potato cakes, or plainly cooked meats, and delicious as a snack or light meal with a poached or fried egg or two on top, or with sautéed mushrooms.

½ small head Savoy or winter cabbage, stems and ribs removed, sliced
olive oil
1 shallot, diced
1 rasher smoked bacon, diced

pinch caraway seeds (optional)
2 tomatoes, peeled, seeded and chopped
salt and freshly ground black pepper
40–55g/1½–2oz Gruyère or Emmenthal cheese, diced

Rinse the cabbage but do not dry it. Put it in a saucepan with a tight-fitting lid and cook for 2–3 minutes, shaking the pan occasionally. Tip into a colander or sieve. Put a little olive oil into the pan, add the shallot and bacon, and cook, stirring occasionally, until the shallot starts to soften. Stir in a small pinch of caraway seeds, if using, and cook until the shallot is soft. Stir in the cabbage and tomatoes. Put on the lid and cook, giving the pan an occasional shake, until the cabbage is just tender, but do not allow it to become too soft. Season with plenty of black pepper but very little salt. Fold in the cheese, then when it is just beginning to melt, spoon the cabbage mixture on to a warmed plate and eat as soon as possible.

Chicory in Foil

Trapped in a foil parcel, the soft cheese bathes the chicory in a creamy sauce. The same technique can be used for many other vegetables.

approximately 40–55g/
  1½–2oz full-fat soft cheese
  flavoured with herbs
1 head chicory

salt and freshly ground black
  pepper
1 tablespoon medium-bodied
  dry white wine or stock
  (optional)

Put about half the cheese on a piece of foil that is large enough to wrap around the chicory. Place the chicory on top, season then top with the remaining cheese. Fold up the sides of the foil, pour in the wine or stock, if using, otherwise substitute water. Seal the edges of the foil tightly. Steam the package in a colander, steaming basket, or on a rack, over boiling water for about 15–20 minutes, depending on how soft you like the chicory to be.

— *Kidney-filled Mushrooms* —

If you are using chopped shallot, spring onion or onion for another dish, fry about 1 heaped teaspoonful of it with the mushroom stalks, for additional flavour.

1 lamb's kidney
salt and freshly ground black
  pepper
unsalted butter, melted
2 large open-cup mushrooms

pinch chopped fresh parsley
cayenne pepper
balsamic or sherry vinegar, or
  lemon juice

Slice the kidney in half and cut away the core, using scissors. Season lightly, brush with a little melted butter then place under a hot grill until browned on the outside but still pink in the centre.

Remove and reserve the mushroom stalks. Brush the caps with melted butter and place under the grill with the kidneys for a few minutes.

Meanwhile, finely chop the mushroom stalks and fry in a little butter until soft. Add a little parsley, season with salt and cayenne pepper and add a dash of balsamic or sherry vinegar, or lemon juice.

Spoon half this mixture into one mushroom cap, place the kidneys on top, top with the remaining mushroom mixture then the other mushroom cap, dome-side uppermost.

VARIATIONS
- Serve on buttered toast, spread, if you like, with garlic purée or mustard.
- Add a little chopped garlic or garlic purée when frying the mushroom stalks.

Mushrooms Topped with Mussels

If you prefer, you can steam rather than grill the mushroom caps. Place them dome-side uppermost on a piece of greaseproof paper, put them on a rack in a steamer or in a colander placed over a saucepan of boiling water, cover and steam for 5 minutes.

2 large cup mushrooms, preferably brown cap (chestnut)
unsalted butter
1 spring onion, finely chopped
salt and freshly ground black pepper
8 fresh mussels removed from their shells (see page 143), or thawed frozen ones
finely chopped fresh herb such as basil, thyme, tarragon or parsley
herb leaves, for garnish (optional)

Remove the stalks from the mushrooms and chop finely. Melt some butter in a small pan, add the chopped mushroom stalks and spring onion and cook gently until tender.

Meanwhile place the mushroom caps dome-side down on a grill rack, season lightly and place a small knob of butter on each cap. Grill for a minute or so, turn over, brush some butter over the dome-side of each cap and grill for another minute or so.

Add the mussels to the pan with the mushroom stalks then add a small sprinkling of chopped herbs and seasoning to taste. Heat through but do not allow to boil.

Place the mushroom caps gill-side uppermost on a warmed plate and spoon on the mussel mixture. Garnish with herb leaves, if liked.

Mushrooms in Oyster Sauce

Oyster sauce has a rich, savoury flavour, not a fishy one. Serve these mushrooms as a vegetable accompaniment to plainly cooked meats, or eat for a first course with good bread to mop up the juice. Any leftover mushrooms keep well in the fridge and can be eaten cold or gently reheated. If the fuller-flavoured brown mushrooms are not available, use ordinary white ones.

mild oil
1 small clove garlic, crushed
approximately 150g/5oz
   brown (chestnut) button
   mushrooms, cut in half if
   large

1 teaspoon dark soy sauce
1½ teaspoons oyster sauce
1½ teaspoons rice wine or dry
   sherry

Heat a little oil in a pan, add the garlic and cook for 30 seconds, stirring. Add the mushrooms, stir-fry for 1 minute, then stir in the remaining ingredients. Reduce the heat so the liquid just simmers then leave to cook for 4–5 minutes, stirring occasionally. If necessary, increase the heat and cook, stirring, until most of the liquid has evaporated.

Sesame Mushrooms

This amount will make one good-sized portion for a first course or for a light meal served with bread, but it may be too much if served as an accompaniment; any that is left can be reheated. Try it spooned on to toast or scrambled eggs or into an omelette, or eat it cold, perhaps with a salad, for a first course.

1 teaspoon peanut oil
½ teaspoon sesame oil
½ teaspoon soy sauce
150g/5oz button mushrooms, halved if large
1 tablespoon rice wine or dry sherry

½–1 tablespoon toasted sesame seeds
freshly ground black pepper
chopped fresh coriander leaves or parsley, for garnish

Heat the oils and soy sauce together in a small nonstick frying pan, add the mushrooms and cook over a high heat for 2–3 minutes, stirring.

Stir in the rice wine or sherry, sprinkle the sesame seeds over the mushrooms and bring to the boil. Cover the pan and simmer for 2–3 minutes. If the mushrooms have given off a lot of liquid, uncover the pan and boil rapidly until the liquid is reduced by half. Add freshly ground black pepper to taste and serve sprinkled with fresh coriander leaves or parsley.

Cheese-stuffed Fennel

Choose a fennel bulb that has only short stalks.

1 fennel bulb
1 small shallot, finely chopped
scant 30g/1oz each crumbled goat's cheese, grated Gruyère or Mozzarella, and Ricotta

freshly ground black pepper
lemon juice, medium-bodied dry white wine or stock (optional)

Remove and reserve any feathery leaves from the fennel. Cut the bulb in half vertically then carefully remove the centre, leaving a 1.25cm/½in shell. Steam the halves over boiling salted water for 10–15 minutes until beginning to soften.

Finely chop the fennel removed from the centre then mix with the shallot, cheeses and black pepper. Divide the filling between the fennel hollows, pressing it down well. Place the halves together and tie firmly with string or strong thread. Place in a lightly oiled dish, sprinkle with a few drops of water, lemon juice, wine or stock, and cover. Bake at 190°C/375°F/gas mark 5 until tender – about 20 minutes. Remove the string before serving.

Lemon-glazed Fennel

1 small fennel bulb
small nut unsalted butter
¾ teaspoon sugar
1 small clove garlic, or garlic
   purée (optional)

2–2½ teaspoons lemon juice
salt and freshly ground white
   pepper
lemon rind, for garnish

Cut off and reserve for garnish any feathery green leaves from the fennel then cut the bulb into 0.5cm/¼in slices.

Melt the butter in a saucepan, stir in the sugar then the fennel slices and the garlic, if using. Cook for 2 minutes, stirring and turning the slices over in the butter. Sprinkle in the lemon juice, cover and cook over a low heat for 3–4 minutes, shaking the pan occasionally.

Remove the lid from the pan, increase the heat to high and cook until the liquid has evaporated and the fennel is just beginning to caramelize; shake the pan occasionally. Season to taste and sprinkle over the lemon rind and reserved chopped fennel leaves.

VARIATIONS
- Braised Fennel with Tomatoes – add 1 skinned, seeded and chopped tomato instead of the lemon juice and cook until the liquid has evaporated.

- Serve either of the above recipes with freshly grated Parmesan cheese sprinkled over.
- Fennel Gratin — sprinkle freshly grated Parmesan cheese mixed with fine breadcrumbs over the top of Braised Fennel with Tomatoes and brown under a hot grill.

Shallot Ragoût

85–115g/3–4oz even-sized shallots
1 small tomato
olive oil or unsalted butter, for cooking

pinch caster sugar
scant teaspoon tomato purée
½ bay leaf
salt and freshly ground black pepper

Peel the shallots, but do not cut through the roots. Skin the tomato, if liked. Remove the seeds and chop the flesh, reserving the juice. Heat a little oil or butter in a small, heavy flameproof casserole. Add the shallots and a pinch of caster sugar, and cook over a moderate heat, stirring occasionally, until the shallots are browned, but do not allow to burn. Stir in 1 tablespoon water then add the tomato and its juice, the tomato purée, bay leaf and seasoning.

Cover and simmer gently, stirring occasionally, for about 10–15 minutes, or until the shallots are just tender but still retain some bite. Add a little more water, if necessary, and adjust the seasoning to taste.

Crisp Parsnip Balls

This recipe makes enough for two servings — keep half of it uncooked, covered, in the refrigerator but remove about 20–30 minutes before cooking. Alternatively open-freeze the uncooked balls until hard then pack in a rigid container, with freezer tissue paper padding out the spaces. Thaw in the refrigerator.

225g/8oz prepared parsnip, diced

15g/½oz unsalted butter or soft cheese

1 small egg, separated

pinch chopped fresh herbs, or small pinch dried herbs

salt and freshly ground black pepper

approximately 55g/2oz unsalted peanuts, finely chopped

groundnut or peanut oil

Steam the parsnips until tender then purée or mash with the butter or cheese, egg yolk, herbs and seasoning. Spread on a plate and leave to cool then divide the mixture into four and form each piece into a ball. Lightly beat the egg white. Coat the balls in the egg white, allowing excess to drain off then coat in the chopped peanuts. Cover and chill.

Fry the balls in hot oil for about 5 minutes until evenly crisp and browned on the outside.

VARIATIONS
- Use salsify or celeriac instead of parsnip.
- Insert a small cube of cheese, a piece of anchovy fillet, garlic sausage, spicy sausage, cooked bacon or ham or some chopped smoked oyster or mussel in the centre of each ball.
- Coat the balls in sesame seeds instead of peanuts.

—————— Parsnips with Chicory Sauce ——————

The slight bitterness of chicory provides a good contrast to the sweetness of parsnips. Serve as an accompaniment, or place on crisp toast for another contrast – that of texture – and another flavour dimension.

Any remaining chicory leaves can be served as a small side

salad with the parsnips and chicory or used in a salad at another meal.

unsalted butter
about 55–85g/2–3oz chicory, very thinly sliced
caster sugar
85ml/3fl oz double cream or fromage blanc

salt and freshly ground black pepper
1 small–medium parsnip, sliced
hot, crisp toast (optional)
nut oil (optional)

Heat a little butter in a saucepan, add the chicory and a small pinch of caster sugar. Cook, stirring, until lightly browned then cover and cook over a low heat for about 15 minutes. If using cream, pour it into the pan, and simmer, uncovered, for about 10 minutes. If using fromage blanc, stir into the chicory and heat gently, but do not allow to boil. Season to taste.

Meanwhile, steam the parsnip until just tender.

If using toast, spread with butter or sprinkle with nut oil, place the parsnips on top then spoon the chicory over and around them.

Salsify with Walnuts

150g/5oz salsify, or scorzonera, cut into 5cm/2in lengths
1 tablespoon walnut oil
1½ teaspoons double cream or Greek yogurt
½–1 teaspoon lemon juice

salt and freshly ground black pepper
1 tablespoon walnuts, roughly chopped and toasted
finely chopped fresh chervil or parsley, for garnish

Steam the salsify or scorzonera over salted water for 6–8 minutes until just tender.

Meanwhile mix the walnut oil and cream or yogurt together

then stir in the lemon juice. Adjust the proportions to taste, and season.

Once the salsify or scorzonera is cooked, refresh it under cold running water and drain well. Using a small knife, remove the skin from each piece. Toss the pieces with the dressing then the walnuts. Garnish with chervil or parsley. Eat warm or cold.

Spiced Celeriac

225g/8oz celeriac
lemon juice
0.5cm/¼in piece root ginger,
    peeled and cut into fine strips
1 small clove garlic, crushed

seeds from 1 cardamom pod
salt and freshly ground black
    pepper
few drops walnut or hazelnut
    oil (optional)

Peel the celeriac then cut into fine strips; to prevent discoloration toss the strips in lemon juice as soon as they have been cut.

Heat a little oil in a heavy pan, add the ginger, garlic and cardamom seeds then cook for 2 minutes, stirring. Stir in the celeriac, coating it in oil then cook, stirring frequently, until softened slightly – or to your taste.

Serve sprinkled with salt and black pepper and a little nut oil, if liked.

Potato and Celeriac Dauphinoise

This dish is just as good cold as it is hot, and as it cooks better in a larger quantity I always make enough for two servings. Leave the uneaten portion to cool, cover and refrigerate until half an hour before it is required then remove from the fridge, uncover and leave to come to room temperature.

Few oven thermostats are accurate at low temperatures, so

keep an eye on how the dauphinoise is cooking. If you would like to use the oven for something else at the same time, try the Rose Cream (see page 221).

approximately 225g/8oz
  celeriac
lemon juice
approximately 225g/8oz
  potatoes
approximately 115ml/4fl oz

milk, single, soured or
  double cream, or a mixture
1 small clove garlic, finely
  crushed
finely grated nutmeg
salt and freshly ground black
  pepper

Peel the celeriac and slice thinly, preferably using a food processor or mandoline then immediately blanch by adding to boiling water acidulated with a squeeze of lemon juice and bringing the water back to the boil. Drain.

Peel the potatoes and slice thinly then layer with the celeriac in a buttered ovenproof dish, pouring a little of the milk or cream over each layer and sprinkling with a little of the garlic, a touch of nutmeg, and seasoning. Finish with a layer of potatoes and pour over the last of the milk or cream. Cook at 170°C/325°F/gas mark 3 for about 1¼–1½ hours, or until very tender. Place the dish under a preheated grill to brown the top if necessary.

—— *Potatoes with Hazelnut Sauce* ——

150g/5oz new potatoes
hazelnut oil
1 tablespoon hazelnuts,
  skinned

2 tablespoons crème fraîche or
  double cream
salt and freshly ground black
  pepper
lemon juice

Steam the potatoes, unpeeled, until tender.

Meanwhile heat about 1 tablespoon hazelnut oil in a pan, add the hazelnuts and cook, stirring, until browned. Using a slotted spoon, transfer to absorbent kitchen paper to drain then crush roughly with a rolling pin, the flat of a wide-bladed knife, or in a pestle and mortar. Add the cooked potatoes to the pan and cook over a fairly high heat, shaking the pan occasionally, until browned and crisp on the outside. Remove using a slotted spoon. Stir another 2 teaspoons oil into the pan, heat then stir in the crème fraîche or cream and boil hard until reduced to a thick pouring sauce. Add seasoning and lemon juice to taste. Pour the sauce over the potatoes and scatter the nuts on top.

Baby Turnips with Orange Butter and Hazelnuts

15g/½oz unsalted butter
1 teaspoon olive oil
1 spring onion, finely chopped
approximately 175g/6oz baby turnips, peeled but left whole

85ml/3fl oz orange juice
salt and freshly ground black pepper
approximately 1 tablespoon lightly toasted chopped hazelnuts, to serve

Melt the butter in a saucepan that is just large enough to hold the turnips in a single layer. Add the oil then the spring onion and cook, stirring occasionally, until the onion is very soft, but do not allow it to colour. Add the turnips and turn them over in the butter and oil. Cook uncovered until they begin to absorb the butter and oil, then add the orange juice. Cook gently for 20–25 minutes, turning the turnips in the liquid occasionally, until they are just tender and the sauce has become slightly syrupy. Add a little more orange juice if the liquid begins to evaporate too fast. Season to taste and scatter the hazelnuts over.

FISH AND SHELLFISH

I make no apologies for including in this chapter quite a number of recipes for ingredients that are usually thought of as luxuries, such as salmon and prawns. In fact these are not as expensive now as they used to be, and obviously it is cheaper to buy just enough for one person than it is to buy large quantities. There is a great temptation for single cooks to 'make do' with snacks, and an occasional treat is a good psychological boost.

Cod with Anchovy Butter

A cool tomato, cucumber, and watercress or spinach salad and a slice of fresh Granary bread or toast complement the savoury flavour of this dish.

lemon juice
approximately 150g/5oz cod
    fillet
olive oil
30g/1oz unsalted butter

scant teaspoon capers,
    chopped
scant teaspoon anchovy paste,
    or to taste
freshly ground black pepper
parsley sprig, for garnish

Sprinkle a little lemon juice over the cod, brush with a little olive oil then cook under a preheated moderately hot grill for about 3 minutes a side.

Meanwhile, mix the butter with the capers, anchovy paste, black pepper, and lemon juice to taste.

Top the cooked fish with the savoury butter, garnish with a sprig of parsley and eat immediately.

VARIATION
• Flavour the butter with Anchoïaide instead (see page 241).

Cod with a Crisp Topping and Garlic Sauce

The crisp topping keeps the fish moist and provides a contrast to the succulent flesh and the creamy sauce, which is quickly made from prepared mayonnaise.

2 tablespoons lemon juice
2 teaspoons olive oil
1 teaspoon finely chopped fresh parsley
salt and freshly ground black pepper
approximately 150g/5oz cod steak

2 tablespoons fresh breadcrumbs
2 tablespoons freshly grated Parmesan cheese
1 tablespoon mayonnaise
garlic purée
parsley sprig and a lemon wedge, to serve

Mix the lemon juice, olive oil, parsley and seasoning together, pour over the cod in a shallow dish and leave, if possible, for 30 minutes.

Remove the cod from the marinade, allowing the excess to drain off and gently scraping off the parsley into the marinade. Pat the fish dry. Mix the breadcrumbs with the Parmesan, stir into the marinade then use to cover the top of the fish evenly.

Cook under a moderate grill until the coating is golden and the fish tender.

Just before the fish is ready, stir 2 teaspoons boiling water into the mayonnaise and add garlic purée to taste.

Transfer the cod to a warmed plate, garnish with the parsley and lemon, and spoon the sauce on to one side.

Cod with Tomato and Walnut Sauce

Tomatoes and walnuts are a magical combination. In this recipe, they are used to make a delicious sauce to which lightly cooked fish is added and the cooking completed.

olive oil
1 small onion, thinly sliced
40g/1½oz walnuts, chopped
1 small tomato, preferably
   skinned, sliced

2 teaspoons finely chopped
   fresh parsley
salt and freshly ground black
   pepper
approximately 175g/6oz cod
   steak or cutlet

Heat a little olive oil in a small pan, add the onion and cook until soft and just beginning to turn golden brown. Add the walnuts and cook for another couple of minutes then add the tomato and cook gently until it has softened. Add the parsley and just enough water to cover. Simmer for a few minutes then season to taste. Cover and keep warm over a very low heat.

Season the cod then fry quickly and lightly on both sides in a little very hot oil. Drain on absorbent kitchen paper. Alternatively, brush the fish with a little oil and grill lightly on both sides. Add the fish to the tomato and walnut sauce, cover and cook very gently for about 5 minutes, or until the fish is opaque.

Fish in Coconut Marinade

Use any firm-texture white fish, such as monkfish, haddock, halibut or cod, cut into steaks, or into cubes for kebabs. Alternatively use prawns.

If you do not have a small blender, pound the shallot and garlic to a paste in a pestle and mortar then work in the spices followed by the coconut and water. Lastly blend in the lime or lemon juice.

55g/2oz block creamed
 coconut, chopped
1 small shallot, finely chopped
1 small clove garlic, finely
 crushed
½ teaspoon ground cardamom
 seeds

2 tablespoons lime or lemon
 juice
¼ teaspoon ground chilli
 powder, or dash chilli sauce,
 or Tabasco sauce
about 150–175g/5–6oz firm-
 textured white fish
 (prepared weight)

Put the coconut into a small blender, add 2 tablespoons boiling water and leave for 2–3 minutes until softened. Add the shallot, garlic, ground cardamom, and lime or lemon juice, and blend until smooth. Add the chilli powder, or chilli sauce or Tabasco sauce to taste, bearing in mind that it will taste more fiery when hot.

Put the fish into a dish, pour the marinade over, stir briefly to coat then leave to marinate for 30 minutes to 1½ hours, depending on the thickness of the fish.

Remove from the marinade, allowing the excess to drain off then cook as appropriate: grill kebabs for 7–9 minutes, turning frequently, or grill steaks for about 6 minutes a side. Serve with the remaining marinade.

Halibut Cooked in Milk

Halibut is a tasty fish, but it can be dry if not cooked sympatheti-
cally. Here, poaching it in milk makes it beautifully moist, then
the milk is used to make a quick and flavourful sauce for an all-
round extremely appetizing dish. Serve with colourful
vegetables.

150ml/5fl oz milk
salt and freshly ground black
  pepper
approximately 150–175g/
  5–6oz halibut cutlet or steak
approximately 4 tablespoons
  breadcrumbs
approximately 40–55g/
  1½–2oz full-fat soft cheese
  flavoured with herbs and
  garlic
lemon juice (optional)
fresh herb sprigs, for garnish

Pour the milk into a small pan in which the fish will just fit,
season lightly and bring to the boil. Add the fish and immediately
reduce the heat so the liquid barely simmers. Cover and cook for
about 8–10 minutes.

Using a fish slice, transfer the fish to a warmed plate and keep
warm. Stir the breadcrumbs into the milk and boil gently for 3–4
minutes until lightly thickened. Stir in soft cheese a little at a
time, to taste, add any juices that have collected on the plate
with the fish, and season with salt, pepper and lemon juice if
necessary. Pour over the fish and garnish with herb sprigs.

VARIATIONS

- Sauté a little chopped shallot or garlic in the pan before adding
  the milk.
- Replace the herb-flavoured cheese with a plain one and add
  fresh herbs to the sauce.

Herring Roes with Grapes

1 tablespoon olive oil
15g/½oz unsalted butter
1 small courgette, sliced
approximately 55g/2oz
  seedless white grapes,
  halved if large
115g/4oz soft herring roes
1 tablespoon lime juice

pinch chopped fresh tarragon,
  or small pinch dried
  tarragon
salt and freshly ground black
  pepper
crisp lettuce and hot toast or
  oatcakes, to serve (optional)

Heat the oil and butter in a frying pan, add the courgette slices and cook, stirring occasionally, until beginning to brown. Push the courgette to one side of the pan and scatter the grapes over it.

Add the herring roes to the free side of the pan and cook over a moderately low heat, stirring occasionally, for 3–4 minutes. Add the lime juice, tarragon and seasoning then carefully stir the roes, courgettes and grapes together.

Serve on a small bed of crisp lettuce and accompanied by hot toast or oatcakes, if liked.

Herring Coated in Oats with Mustard Sauce

Herring is a much underrated fish – when it is fresh it ranks among the best. The crisp coating makes a good contrast to the soft richness of the fish.

approximately 4 tablespoons
   soured cream or Greek
   yogurt
mustard e.g. Dijon, Bordeaux,
   wholegrain
salt and freshly ground black
   pepper
2 herring fillets
lemon juice

1 small egg white, lightly
   beaten
scant teaspoon coarsely
   crushed black peppercorns
approximately 1½–2
   tablespoons rolled oats
oil or butter
salt
lemon wedge, to serve

Flavour the soured cream or Greek yogurt with mustard and seasoning to taste. Sprinkle the fish with a little lemon juice and rub it in well. Dip the fillets in the egg white and allow the excess to drain off. Mix the crushed black peppercorns with the rolled oats on a plate then coat the fish evenly in the mixture, pressing it on quite firmly.

Heat a little oil or butter in a frying pan, add the fish and cook until crisp and brown, turning once.

Drain on absorbent kitchen paper. Sprinkle with salt and serve with the mustard sauce and a wedge of lemon to squeeze over.

Smoked Mackerel with Peppered Cream

6 black peppercorns
approximately ½ teaspoon
   horseradish cream, to taste
2 tablespoons crème fraîche,

soured cream or Greek
   yogurt, chilled
1 smoked mackerel fillet,
   flaked
crisp lettuce leaves, chilled

Roast the peppercorns in a small, heavy pan over a high heat until they start to brown and pop. Remove from the pan, allow to cool then either crush finely or put into a pepper-grinder.

Add sufficient horseradish cream to the crème fraîche, soured cream or yogurt to flavour it quite mildly then add the crushed or ground black peppercorns.

Place the flaked mackerel on a baking tray or piece of foil under a low grill to warm through thoroughly without the fat oozing then spoon a little mackerel on to each lettuce leaf, top with the dressing, roll up and eat immediately. Keep the remaining mackerel covered to keep it warm as you make the rolls.

VARIATION
● Buy a peppered mackerel fillet and flavour the yogurt or soured cream with mustard.

———— Monkfish and Bacon Kebabs ————

This is a very useful, adaptable basic recipe because more or less any type of herb or citrus fruit can be used, thereby changing the character of the dish quite considerably.

1 tablespoon olive oil
2 teaspoons finely grated lime or lemon rind
2 teaspoons lime or lemon juice
approximately 4 teaspoons chopped mixed fresh herbs – parsley, thyme, marjoram, tarragon, basil, dill, fennel etc.

salt and freshly ground black pepper
approximately 175g/6oz monkfish fillet, cut into approximately 2cm/¾in cubes
1 clove garlic
2 bacon rashers, cut in half

In a shallow dish mix together the oil, lime or lemon rind and juice, herbs and seasoning, adding only a little salt because of the saltiness of the bacon. Add the monkfish, turning the cubes over to coat them in the dressing. If time allows, leave for about half an hour.

Run one or two skewers, depending on their length, through the garlic clove. Discard the clove (or use in another recipe).

Roll the bacon pieces up neatly. Remove the monkfish from the dressing, allowing the excess to drain off, then thread the monkfish and the bacon rolls alternately on the skewers. Brush the bacon with the dressing and grill the kebabs under a moderate grill for about 8–10 minutes, turning them so they cook evenly and brushing occasionally with the dressing. Serve with any remaining dressing.

VARIATION
● Substitute other firm-fleshed fish for the monkfish, such as tuna or salmon.

Monkfish and Prosciutto Morsels

In this recipe, the not uncommon practice of wrapping fish such as monkfish or prawns in bacon is taken one stage further. Fine slices of prosciutto (raw, air-dried Italian ham) are substituted for the bacon, and protected by a coating of egg, flour and breadcrumbs, making cooked morsels that are a series of contrasting textures and flavours in the mouth. A deep-fat frying pan is not necessary – use a pan that is large enough to hold a good depth of oil and use a slotted spoon to lower the cubes into and remove them from the oil.

2–3 slices prosciutto
approximately 85–115g/3–4oz
  monkfish fillet, cubed
approximately 2 rounded
  tablespoons flour
salt and freshly ground black
  pepper

1 small egg
approximately 3 rounded
  tablespoons fresh
  breadcrumbs
oil
tartar sauce and lemon
  wedges, to serve

Cut the prosciutto into pieces large enough to enclose a piece of monkfish then wrap up the fish. Lightly season the flour then coat the wrapped monkfish in a light covering.

Beat the egg in a small bowl, dip the monkfish cubes in the egg then allow the excess to drain off. Lastly, coat with breadcrumbs.

Fry the morsels in a good depth of hot oil until golden and crisp on the outside but still tender and moist in the centre – about 2–3 minutes.

Transfer to absorbent kitchen paper to drain then eat hot with tartar sauce and a squeeze of lemon.

VARIATIONS
- Use ground almonds instead of breadcrumbs.
- Spread a dab of pesto on the fish.
- Sprinkle Tabasco sauce on the fish.
- Use queen scallops or halved ordinary scallops in place of monkfish and cook for slightly less time.

———— Monkfish Braised with Fennel ————

Monkfish has become popular only in the last few years, and unfortunately as its popularity has increased so has its price. It is well worth buying, though, as it has a good flavour and texture and only one large, central bone – the ideal fish for people who are put off by fiddly and treacherous bones.

Make sure all the fine membrane on the monkfish tail has

been removed, otherwise it will contract during cooking, spoiling the shape of the tail.

approximately 300–350g/
   10–12oz monkfish tail
lemon juice
salt and freshly ground black
   pepper

1 small fennel bulb
30g/1oz unsalted butter
1 tablespoon Aïoli (see page
   239), or garlic-flavoured
   mayonnaise

With the point of a small sharp knife, make small incisions in the tail then rub lemon juice into the flesh and season. Cut the fennel vertically into quarters, cut off the feathery tops and chop them. Slice the quartered bulb thinly then place the slices in an ovenproof casserole into which the monkfish tail will just fit. Dot with half the butter, place the fish on top and dot with the remaining butter. Squeeze a little lemon juice over.

Cover and bake for about 15–20 minutes at 180°C/350°F/gas mark 4, basting with the juices about three times.

Using a fish slice, transfer the monkfish and fennel to a warmed serving plate and keep warm. Stir a little of the cooking juices into the aïoli or mayonnaise then pour this mixture into the casserole dish. Heat through on top of the stove but do not boil. Test for seasoning, and add a little more lemon juice, if necessary. Spoon alongside the fish and sprinkle with the chopped fennel top.

VARIATION
● If you do not have any aïoli or garlic-flavoured mayonnaise, add ¼–½ finely chopped garlic clove or about ¼ teaspoon garlic purée to 1 tablespoon mayonnaise.

——— *Monkfish with Garlic and Tomatoes* ———

This recipe demonstrates how useful a good-quality store-cupboard mayonnaise can be for making a quick, creamy hot sauce. If you have some homemade mayonnaise in the fridge you could use that instead, but allow it to come to room temperature before heating it. Serve with good bread to mop up the flavourful juices.

3 medium tomatoes, peeled, seeded and chopped
1 tablespoon finely chopped shallot
1 small clove garlic, chopped
2 teaspoons chopped fresh parsley
4 tablespoons medium-bodied dry white wine (optional)

approximately 175g/6oz skinned monkfish fillet
2 tablespoons good-quality mayonnaise
salt and freshly ground black pepper
2 parsley sprigs, for garnish

Put the tomatoes, shallot, garlic, chopped parsley and wine, if using, in a pan that is just large enough to hold the fish. Lay the fish in the pan, bring to simmering point, cover and cook for about 3 minutes.

Using a fish slice, transfer the monkfish to a warmed serving plate. Boil the liquid over a moderate heat until reduced by about three-quarters. Add any juices that have collected on the plate with the monkfish, bring to simmering point again then remove from the heat and whisk in the mayonnaise. Season to taste.

Pour the sauce over the monkfish and garnish with the parsley sprigs.

Monkfish and Mussel Kebabs

The sweet flesh of monkfish and tangy mussels make a good combination and both are enhanced by olive oil, lemon or lime juice and herbs. They also look very attractive on skewers together.

1 clove garlic
approximately 115g/4oz
   monkfish fillet, cut into
   2.5cm/1in cubes
6 thawed frozen mussels
2 teaspoons virgin olive oil
4 teaspoons chopped fresh
   mixed herbs – parsley,

marjoram, chervil, thyme,
   basil
1 teaspoon lime or lemon rind
1 tablespoon lime or lemon
   juice
salt and freshly ground black
   pepper

Thread the garlic clove on a skewer and run it up and down several times. If using two skewers, repeat with the second one. Discard the garlic (or use in another recipe). Thread the monkfish and mussels alternately on the skewer or skewers. Mix the oil, herbs, lime or lemon rind and juice and seasoning together in a small bowl and use to brush the fish. Place on an oiled grill rack and cook under a moderate grill, turning frequently and brushing with the herb mixture, for 5–8 minutes until the fish is just cooked.

VARIATION
- If the only fresh herb available is parsley, which it may be in winter, use just 3 teaspoonfuls plus a few crushed fennel or dill seeds.

Mussels with Black Bean Cream Sauce

Golden-yellow fresh mussels with the salty tang of the sea have a definite edge over frozen ones but, whereas shucking enough for 4 people can be very laborious, and take so long that it hardly seems worth the effort, preparing them for a single portion is not only bearable but rewarding, and one of the advantages of cooking for one.

500g/1lb/1 pint fresh mussels in their shells, or 150g/5oz frozen mussels, thawed
1 small shallot, finely chopped
3 tablespoons medium-bodied dry white wine
1 tablespoon chopped Chinese fermented black beans (available in cans)
2 tablespoons crème fraîche or Greek yogurt
freshly ground black pepper
1 small tomato, skinned, seeds removed and chopped
approximately 1 teaspoon finely chopped fresh parsley
1 tablespoon fish stock, if using frozen mussels (optional)

Clean fresh mussels as follows: soak in salted water with 1 tablespoon oatmeal or flour for 1–2 hours to rid them of grit. Scrub the shells and pull out and cut off the stringy beards. Rinse the shells well.

If using fresh mussels, put the shallot and wine into a wide pan and bring to simmering point. Add the mussels, cover the pan, bring to the boil then simmer for 4–5 minutes until the mussel shells open.

Remove the mussels from the liquid, allowing any liquid in the shells to drain back into the pan. Discard any mussels that remain closed. Remove the mussels from the open shells.

Strain the cooking liquid into a small pan and boil until reduced to 1 tablespoon. Stir in the beans, heat for about 30 seconds then, over a low heat, stir in the crème fraîche or yogurt and the mussels, season and heat through – do not allow the sauce to boil if using yogurt. Stir in the chopped tomato and serve with the parsley sprinkled over.

If using frozen mussels, boil the shallot in the wine and fish stock, if using, otherwise add 1 tablespoon water, and boil until reduced to about 1 tablespoon. Continue as above.

En Papillote

Cooking fish in a foil or greaseproof paper parcel is a good – and easy – way of keeping it moist and trapping its juices and flavour. It is also simple to add additional flavourings, such as sprigs of fresh herbs, chopped herbs, capers or olives, lemon or lime juice, a couple of tablespoons of medium-dry white wine, or a tablespoon of dry white vermouth, diced vegetables such as tomatoes, shallots, mushrooms, courgettes and a small knob of butter, or soft cheese (one flavoured with herbs and garlic flavours the fish as well), if liked.

Brill Baked with Tomatoes and Mushrooms

1 small shallot or spring onion
salt and freshly ground black pepper
approximately 175g/6oz brill fillet
1 medium-sized tomato, preferably skinned, seeded and chopped

40–55g/1½–2oz mushrooms, thinly sliced
small pinch chopped fresh thyme, fennel, basil or parsley
small knob unsalted butter
herb sprig, to garnish

Scatter the shallot or spring onion over a piece of foil that is large enough to enclose the fish completely. Season both sides of the fish and lay on the shallot or spring onion. Scatter the tomato and mushrooms on the fish, followed by the herb and a little more seasoning. Dot the butter over then fold the foil loosely over the fish, sealing the edges securely. Cook under a hot grill for about 4 minutes then turn the parcel over and cook for a further 4 minutes.

Open the parcel, carefully transfer the fish and vegetables to a warmed serving plate then pour the cooking juices into a small pan and bubble until slightly thickened. Taste, adjust the seasoning and pour over the fish. Garnish with a sprig of herb.

VARIATIONS
- Add about 3 tablespoons medium-bodied dry white wine to the fish before cooking and stir 1 tablespoon double cream into the slightly thickened cooking juices over a low heat.
- Chopped sun-dried tomato can be used instead of or as well as fresh tomato.

Mackerel with Mustard and Coriander

The well-known successful combination of mackerel and mustard is given a new twist, and more impact, by the inclusion of fresh coriander.

2 teaspoons mustard
1 tablespoon finely chopped
  fresh coriander leaves
1 small clove garlic, finely
  crushed
lemon juice

salt and freshly ground black
  pepper
1 mackerel, gutted and
  cleaned
rolled oats or breadcrumbs

Mix the mustard, coriander, garlic, a little lemon juice, and seasoning together. Using the point of a sharp knife, make 3 slashes in each side of the mackerel. Spoon the mustard mixture into the slashes and sprinkle a few oats or breadcrumbs over. Wrap the fish in foil, sealing the joins tightly then place under a preheated hot grill for about 5 minutes. Open the foil, turn the fish over, reseal the package and grill for a further 2–3 minutes. Open the foil, place nearer the heat and cook for another 2 minutes or so.

Mackerel with Lemon, Garlic and Rosemary

1 tablespoon olive oil
1 clove garlic, chopped
1 mackerel, cleaned but with
    the head and tail left on
small sprig fresh rosemary, or
    small pinch dried rosemary

2 teaspoons lemon juice
salt and freshly ground black
    pepper
lemon wedge, to serve

Heat the oil in a heavy pan or flameproof casserole, add the garlic and cook for 2 minutes. Add the mackerel and rosemary, lower the heat to medium and cook, turning once, until the fish is brown on both sides, but do not allow it to stick. Pour the lemon juice over the fish, add the seasoning, and cover the pan tightly. Reduce the heat to very low and cook the mackerel gently for about 15 minutes or until tender.

Transfer the mackerel to a warmed serving plate, taste the cooking juices and add a little lemon juice or seasoning, if necessary then spoon them over the fish. Serve with a wedge of lemon.

Smoked Mackerel with Apple and Sesame Seeds

The sharpness of the fruit juices and the crispness of the apple and salad leaves make a wonderful contrast to the richness of the mackerel.

crisp salad leaves
2 tablespoons apple juice
1 teaspoon virgin olive oil
lime or lemon juice
freshly ground white or black
   pepper

1 smoked mackerel fillet,
   skinned and roughly flaked
1 small, crisp apple, cored and
   sliced or chopped
toasted sesame seeds

Arrange the salad leaves on a plate. Whisk the apple juice and oil together then add lime or lemon juice and pepper to taste.

Toss the mackerel and apple together, place on the lettuce and spoon the dressing over. Toss lightly then sprinkle with sesame seeds.

VARIATION
- Substitute approximately 55g/2oz smoked eel for the mackerel.

—— *Prawns with Mint and Avocado* ——

Mint and pastis are a surprisingly good combination, and together they give a new, sophisticated taste to the perennial favourite – avocado and prawns.

1½ tablespoons mayonnaise
2 teaspoons soured cream,
   crème fraîche, Greek yogurt
   or fromage blanc
pastis
lemon juice

5 fresh mint leaves, plus 1
   sprig for garnish
55g/2oz peeled prawns, chilled
1 small avocado
lettuce leaves (optional)
grated lemon or lime rind

Mix the mayonnaise and soured cream, crème fraîche, yogurt or fromage blanc together then stir in pastis and lemon juice to taste.

Tear the mint leaves into small pieces and mix with the prawns.

Peel the avocado, slice the flesh and immediately either toss in lemon juice or brush the surfaces with lemon juice.

Shred the lettuce leaves, if using, and arrange on a plate. Lay the avocado on top, scatter the prawns and mint over and spoon the dressing into the centre. Garnish with a small sprig of mint and the grated lemon or lime rind.

VARIATIONS

- To serve the avocado in the more conventional way, cut it in half, remove the stone then fill the cavity with the prawns and spoon the dressing on top.
- If you do not have fresh mint, infuse ½ teaspoon dried mint in 1 teaspoon pastis for 1–6 hours then strain off the liquid and mix into the mayonnaise sauce.
- Prawns with Mint and Melon – use melon balls instead of avocado.

Fiery Prawns

Real chilli can be used instead of Tabasco sauce, but a word of caution about the preparation of chillies, both fresh and dried – their flesh and seeds contain volatile oils that can make the eyes sting and the skin tingle, so do not touch your face or eyes when preparing them; you can wear rubber gloves for protection but this does make preparation a little difficult. Add just part of the chilli to start with then you can easily add some more if you want a hotter flavour.

Serve with rice and a crisp green salad.

3 raw Mediterranean prawns,
or 5 large prawns
1 tablespoon olive oil
1 clove garlic, chopped
2 tomatoes, skinned, deseeded
and chopped

Tabasco sauce
salt and freshly ground black
pepper
wedge of lime or lemon, to
serve (optional)

Remove the shells from the prawns, leaving the heads in place.

Heat the oil in a small pan, add the garlic and cook for 1–2 minutes. Stir in the tomatoes and a drop or two of Tabasco sauce and simmer gently, stirring occasionally, until the tomatoes have disintegrated – about 5 minutes. Stir in the prawns and simmer gently for 1–2 minutes until the prawns are lightly cooked. Season and adjust the levels of flavour. Serve with a wedge of lime, if available, or lemon.

——— *Prawns with Fresh Coriander* ———

If you are not able to buy raw prawns, use cooked ones and stir them in when most of the liquid has evaporated, so that they just warm through without toughening.

unsalted butter
olive oil
175g/6oz raw prawns
1 small clove garlic, finely
chopped
1 tablespoon rice wine or dry
sherry

4 tablespoons fish stock or
water
2 teaspoons Dijon mustard
2 teaspoons finely chopped
fresh coriander

Heat the butter and oil in a frying pan, add the prawns and garlic and cook over a high heat, stirring, for 1 minute. Stir in the rice wine or sherry, the fish stock or water, mustard and coriander and cook briefly over a high heat until the prawns are translucent and the excess liquid has evaporated. Serve immediately.

Jumbo Prawns with Basil Tabbouleh

Any, or all, of the various stages of this summery light lunch dish can be prepared in advance.

1–2 heaped tablespoons fresh basil leaves
½ clove garlic, finely chopped
2 tablespoons mild olive oil
3–4 large raw prawns
2 tablespoons fish, vegetable or chicken stock (optional)
small knob unsalted butter, diced

1 slightly rounded tablespoon couscous
1 teaspoon lemon juice
1 small tomato, skinned and chopped
approximately 1.25cm/½in slice cucumber, peeled and chopped

Finely chop the basil leaves then mix in a small bowl with the garlic and olive oil. Bring a little water to the boil in a pan, add the prawns, cover and cook for about 3 minutes. Leave until cool enough to handle then peel. Toss with half of the basil oil. Bring the stock, if using, to the boil with the butter in a small saucepan, remove from the heat then immediately stir in the couscous and lemon juice. Leave for 5 minutes then transfer to a bowl. If not using stock, add the butter to the couscous in a bowl, pour over 2 tablespoons boiling water and stir in the lemon juice. Allow to cool to room temperature.

Stir the remaining basil oil into the couscous then toss in the tomato and cucumber. Form into a 'cake' on a plate and place the prawns on top. Spoon over any oil remaining from the prawns.

VARIATION
- Substitute lightly cooked cubes of salmon for prawns.

——————— *Potted Prawns with Ginger* ———————

Ginger and lime bring traditional potted prawns up to date. Serve with a crisp green salad for a first course or light lunch, or 'pot' the prawns in individual dishes and take as part of a packed lunch or picnic.

115g/4oz cooked shelled prawns

1.25cm/½in piece juicy root ginger, peeled

finely grated rind and juice ½ small lime

115g/4oz unsalted butter, diced

½ small clove garlic, sliced

Roughly chop about a third of the prawns then put both chopped and whole prawns into a bowl. Using a garlic press held over the bowl, squeeze the ginger juices over the prawns. Stir in the lime rind and juice then leave to marinate for about 1 hour, turning the prawns over occasionally. Tip the prawns and juices into 1 bowl, or 2 smaller ones.

Gently melt the butter in a pan with the garlic then allow it to sizzle for 4–5 minutes. Remove the scum from the top of the butter and discard. Carefully pour the clear liquid off the sediment on to the prawns. If necessary, gently push down any prawns that protrude above the surface of the butter so they are completely covered. Leave to cool then cover and chill.

To turn the mould out, dip briefly in very hot water then run the point of a small sharp knife around the inside edge of the dish.

Red Mullet with Lemon and Courgettes

1 shallot, finely chopped
115g/4oz courgette, sliced
1 tomato, preferably skinned, chopped
finely grated rind ½ lemon
1 teaspoon chopped thyme, tarragon, marjoram or mixed herbs
salt and freshly ground black pepper
1 red mullet, about 225–300g/ 8–10oz
lemon juice

Lightly oil a piece of foil that is large enough to enclose the fish completely. Put half the shallot, courgette and tomato on the foil and sprinkle with half the lemon rind and herbs and a little seasoning. Lay the fish on top, cover with the remaining vegetables then sprinkle on the remaining lemon rind and herbs, a little more seasoning and a squeeze of lemon juice. Fold the foil loosely over the fish and seal the joins firmly. Place in a steaming basket, colander or large sieve in a pan of boiling water, cover and steam for about 25 minutes.

VARIATION
● Substitute trout for red mullet.

Red Mullet with Tomato and Tarragon

Another example of how the simplest recipes for fish are often the most successful.

salt and freshly ground black
  pepper
2 red mullet fillets
1 medium-sized tomato,
  peeled, seeded and chopped
small pinch chopped fresh
  tarragon

2 teaspoons finely chopped
  shallot
1½ tablespoons olive oil
1 teaspoon lime juice
tarragon leaves, for garnish

Season both sides of the fillets. Brush the grill rack with a little oil then cook the fish under a preheated moderate grill for about 3 minutes a side until just tender.

Meanwhile in a small bowl mix together the tomato, tarragon, shallot, olive oil, lime juice and seasoning. Place the bowl over a saucepan of hot water and heat through.

Transfer the fish to a warmed plate and spoon the sauce over. Garnish with tarragon leaves.

VARIATIONS
- Substitute lemon juice for lime.
- Substitute trout fillets or brill fillets for red mullet.

Salmon with Cardamom Citrus Dressing

1 tablespoon olive oil
1 teaspoon lime juice
2 teaspoons orange juice
pinch crushed cardamom
  seeds

1 salmon steak
salt and freshly ground black
  pepper

Whisk together the olive oil, lime and orange juices and cardamom seeds. Place the salmon in a non-metallic dish, pour the dressing over, cover and leave in the refrigerator overnight.

Drain the salmon and cook under a hot grill for about 4 minutes a side.

Meanwhile pour the marinade into a small saucepan and bring to the boil. Season and keep warm over a low heat until the salmon is cooked. Serve the salmon with the warm dressing poured over.

VARIATION

• Just lime or orange juice can be used instead of the combination, or lemon juice can be substituted.

_____ *Salmon with Tarragon and* _____
Tomato Vinaigrette

1 ½ teaspoons chopped fresh tarragon

½ teaspoon chopped fresh parsley

2 tablespoons extra-virgin olive oil

½–1 teaspoon lime juice

½–1 teaspoon white wine vinegar

½ clove garlic, blanched in a little boiling water for 1 minute and cut into fine strips

salt and freshly ground black pepper

1 salmon steak

1 large tomato, skinned, seeds removed, chopped

tarragon sprigs, for garnish

Mix the first seven ingredients together. Place the salmon in a shallow, non-metallic dish, spoon about a tablespoon of the dressing over and leave to marinate in a cool place for up to 2 hours. If there is no time for this, simply brush the fish with the dressing.

· Remove the salmon from the marinade, allowing the excess to drain off, and cook under a hot grill for about 3–4 minutes a side. Mix the tomato into the dressing.

Spoon the dressing over the fish and garnish with tarragon sprigs.

VARIATIONS
- Substitute 2 trout fillets for the salmon and reduce the cooking time to 1½–2½ minutes per side.
- Replace the salmon with a tuna steak.
- Use other herbs in place of tarragon, such as basil, mint or chives.

———— *Salmon with Watercress* ————

The watercress is puréed and then some of the purée is placed on a plate to make a contrasting bed for the rich salmon. The rest is made into a more muted, pretty green sauce that is poured around and over the salmon.

unsalted butter
1 tablespoon finely chopped shallot
1 salmon steak
1 bunch or pack watercress, about 115g/4oz
salt and freshly ground black pepper

55ml/2fl oz fish stock, or water
55ml/2fl oz medium-bodied dry white wine (optional)
2 tablespoons double cream, fromage blanc or Greek yogurt

Heat a little butter in a pan, add the shallot and cook over a moderate heat, stirring occasionally, until softened. Add the salmon and cook for about 3–4 minutes a side.

Meanwhile, remove and discard the thick stalks from the watercress. Drop the watercress in a bowl of boiling water, leave for 1 minute then drain. Rinse under cold running water, drain thoroughly then purée. Spread half of the purée on a warmed serving plate.

Remove the salmon from the pan, season and place on the watercress on the warmed plate. Cover and keep warm.

Stir the stock or water into the pan and boil until reduced by half. Add the wine, if using, and reduce the liquid by half again. Lower the heat and stir in the cream, fromage blanc or Greek yogurt then the remaining watercress purée. Adjust the seasoning and spoon the sauce over and around the salmon.

VARIATION
● Trout with Watercress – use 1 whole trout or 2 fillets instead of the salmon.

Medallions of Salmon with Basil Sauce

A dish for summer months when fresh basil is at its most aromatic. Its flavour disappears quickly, so do not tear the leaves until just before they are needed, and do not chop them as this damages their fragile structure, expelling their essential fragrant oil.

1 salmon steak	lemon juice
unsalted butter	salt and freshly ground black
3 tablespoons fish stock	pepper
(optional)	lemon wedges or twists, to
3 tablespoons double cream	serve
3 fresh basil leaves	

Carefully cut away the central bone from the salmon then cut the steak in half lengthways. Carefully remove the skin from each piece then curl the flesh around to give 2 medallions. Tie into shape with thread or fine string.

Melt a little butter in a small frying pan, add the salmon and cook briskly on both sides for about 1½ minutes. Add the stock, if using, otherwise add 2 tablespoons of water, and the cream. Heat just to simmering then transfer the salmon to a warmed plate. Simmer the cream for 2 minutes, lower the heat and add the basil leaves, torn into 3 pieces each, and lemon juice and seasoning to taste. Pour any juices that have collected on the plate with the salmon into the sauce. Remove the thread or string from the salmon, pour the sauce over the fish and serve with wedges or twists of lemon.

VARIATION

● Flavour the sauce with a little pesto to taste instead of fresh basil.

Sea Bass with Lemon and Chive Sauce

Sea bass is highly prized, and much in demand by restaurants. Unfortunately, this and the fact that catches are restricted mean it is expensive. However, attempts are being made to farm it, so hopefully it will soon become more readily available and more affordable. This simple, fresh recipe does it full justice.

1 tablespoon olive oil, or small nut unsalted butter
150–175g/5–6oz sea bass fillet
55ml/2fl oz medium-bodied dry white wine or fish stock (optional)
rind from ¼ lemon, cut into fine strips
2–3 teaspoons lemon juice

2 teaspoons white wine vinegar
55ml/2fl oz olive oil
salt and freshly ground white pepper
small pinch sugar
1 tablespoon chives, very finely chopped

Brush the oil evenly over the fish, or rub butter over it. Place in a small pan into which it just fits and pour in the wine or stock, if using, or substitute water. Cover and bring just to simmering point. Adjust the heat so the liquid barely moves and cook the fish for about 4 minutes or until just tender.

Meanwhile bring the lemon rind to the boil in a small amount
of water in a small saucepan. Drain, refresh under cold running
water and drain again. Whisk together the lemon rind and juice,
vinegar, oil and seasoning. Add a very small pinch of sugar and
adjust the proportions of lemon juice, vinegar and oil to taste, if
necessary. Add the chives.

When the fish is done, use a fish slice or slotted spoon to
transfer it to a warmed serving plate then spoon the dressing
over.

──────── *Scallop and Cucumber Kebabs* ────────

This is a rather self-indulgent recipe as scallops are quite expensive. Their delectable, delicate flavour and texture are worth
every penny, though, and if you are feeling a little miserable, the
clean, fresh flavours and contrasting textures of this dish are
bound to cheer you up.

1 teaspoon finely chopped
  fresh dill, or small pinch
  dried dill
2 teaspoons lemon juice
generous tablespoon olive oil
salt and freshly ground black
  pepper
4–8 fresh scallops, depending

on size, removed from their
  shells, and sliced in half
  horizontally if large
approximately 5cm/2in piece
  cucumber
sprig of fresh dill, to serve
  (optional)
lemon wedge, to serve

Mix together the chopped dill, lemon juice, oil and seasoning in
a non-metallic bowl. Stir in the scallops, cover and leave to
marinate for 15–60 minutes.

Peel the cucumber, cut it in half then scoop out and discard
the seeds and cut the flesh into 8 pieces. Blanch in boiling water
for 30 seconds, refresh, drain and pat dry.

Remove the scallops from the marinade, allowing the excess

to drain off. Thread the scallops and cucumber alternately on to skewers then cook under a moderately hot grill for about 5–8 minutes, turning and basting frequently with the marinade. Serve with any remaining marinade spooned over, garnish with a sprig of dill, if available, and add a lemon wedge.

VARIATIONS
- Substitute mint for the dill.
- Use monkfish fillet cut into cubes, or prawns, instead of scallops.

———— *Skate with Lemon and Anchovy* ————

Skate is one of several fish that have recently become far more widely available. It is quick to cook, sweet-tasting and easy to eat as there are no small bones to contend with.

salt and freshly ground black pepper
approximately 200g/7oz piece skate
2 teaspoons olive oil
very small nut unsalted butter
1 anchovy fillet, soaked in milk for 10 minutes, drained and cut into strips
approximately 1 tablespoon lemon juice
2 teaspoons capers
2 teaspoons chopped fresh parsley, for garnish (optional)
lemon wedges or twists, for garnish

Season the skate. Heat the oil and butter together in a frying pan, add the skate and cook over a moderate heat until golden on both sides. Using a slotted spoon, transfer to a warmed plate. Lay the strips of anchovy fillet over the fish.

Stir the lemon juice into the cooking juices. Bring to the boil, add the capers then pour over the skate. Sprinkle the parsley over, if using, and garnish with lemon wedges or twists.

Smoked Salmon Parcels

This is delicious served with pumpernickel bread and accompanied by a crisp salad for a light lunch or supper, or simply with a salad garnish for a first course.

55g/2oz hummous
70g/2½oz low-fat soft cheese
1½ teaspoons finely chopped
  fresh coriander

lemon or lime juice
4 large thin slices smoked
  salmon – about 55g/2oz
lemon or lime wedges

Beat the hummous and soft cheese together then add the coriander and lemon or lime juice to taste.

Lay out the smoked salmon slices, divide the hummous mixture between them and fold the salmon over to make parcels. Place with the loose ends underneath and serve with a couple of lime or lemon wedges.

VARIATION
• Flavour the hummous with a touch of horseradish and omit the coriander.

Trout in Foil with Tomato, Olives and Anchovy

This combination of ingredients is redolent of the Mediterranean and transforms a simple trout into a richly flavoured dish.

1 tablespoon olive oil
1 small shallot, finely chopped
1 small clove garlic, finely
    chopped
salt and freshly ground black
    pepper
1 trout, cleaned and gutted
1 small–medium tomato,
    preferably skinned, chopped

1–2 large black olives, stoned
    and sliced
1 small anchovy fillet, soaked
    in a little milk, drained and
    cut into strips
small fennel sprig, or ¼
    teaspoon fennel seeds

Heat the oil in a small pan, add the shallot and garlic and cook over a moderate heat, stirring occasionally, until softened.

Season the trout inside and out and place about half of the shallot mixture in the cavity. Spread about half of the remaining shallot mixture on a sheet of foil that is large enough to enclose the trout completely then place the trout on top of it. Spread the remaining shallot mixture over the trout and scatter the tomato and olives over then place the anchovy strips on top. Top with the fennel sprig or scatter the fennel seeds over. Fold the foil loosely over the fish and secure the edges tightly together.

Place the parcel in a steamer, large colander or fine-meshed rack, cover tightly and steam over simmering water for about 20 minutes or until the trout is tender. Serve straight from the package.

Trout with Tahina

Tahina is a sesame seed paste that can be bought in jars from healthfood shops, delicatessens or good supermarkets. Once opened, the paste will keep for a long time if stored in the refrigerator.

approximately 1 tablespoon
tahina

approximately 2–3 teaspoons
lemon juice

salt and freshly ground black
pepper

2 trout fillets

toasted pine nuts or flaked
almonds

Mix the tahina with the lemon juice and seasoning – the tahina will go sticky and crumbly at first then, as more lemon juice is added, it turns to a smooth cream. Lay the trout fillets skin-side uppermost in a heatproof dish. Cook under a moderately hot grill for about 3–4 minutes then turn the fish over, spread with the tahina paste, and cook under a moderate grill for a further 5 minutes or so. Serve with the nuts scattered over.

VARIATION
● Flavour the tahina with a pinch of cumin seeds or ground cumin.

Tuna in Ginger Vinaigrette

Tuna is a fine-flavoured, firm-textured fish, which is best lightly cooked to preserve its succulence. If you are lucky enough to have a really fresh tuna steak it can be given the briefest of cooking to leave it still 'rare' in the centre.

½–1 teaspoon finely chopped
fresh root ginger

scant teaspoon rice vinegar

1 tablespoon olive oil

approximately ½ teaspoon
each sesame oil and soy
sauce

approximately 1½ teaspoons
lime juice

salt and freshly ground black
pepper

approximately 150g/5oz fresh
tuna steak

1 tablespoon chopped fresh
coriander or flat-leaved
parsley

½–1 teaspoon lightly toasted
sesame seeds

coriander or flat-leaved
parsley sprigs, for garnish

Mix together the ginger, vinegar, oils, soy sauce, lime juice and seasoning, adjusting the proportions to taste.

Lay the fish in a shallow, non-metallic dish, spoon a little of the dressing over and leave to marinate in a cool place for up to 2 hours, turning the fish over once or twice.

Remove the fish from the marinade, allowing the excess to drain off. Cook under a hot grill for about 2–3 minutes a side, or longer, depending on the freshness of the fish and your preference.

Stir the chopped coriander or parsley into the remaining dressing.

To serve, spoon the dressing on to a plate, put the fish on top and sprinkle with the sesame seeds. Garnish with coriander or parsley sprigs.

VARIATIONS

- Substitute 2 trout fillets for the tuna and reduce the cooking time to 1½–2½ minutes a side.
- Substitute a salmon steak or fillet for the tuna.

Poultry

Grilled Poultry

Quick and easy ways to flavour grilled poultry:
- Baste during cooking with oil and lemon, lime or orange juice flavoured with fresh or dried herbs, such as rosemary, fennel, thyme, tarragon, basil, chives, marjoram and oregano.
- Marinate in oil with lemon, lime, orange or apple juice and chopped herbs or crushed seeds, such as fennel and dill, or spices. Marinades penetrate more quickly if the meat is at room temperature rather than in the fridge; if the meat has been skinned; if you are using a small or thin cut. To speed up the process the flesh can be slashed.
- Marinate in yogurt flavoured with herbs, or paprika or other spices, such as Chinese five-spice powder.
- Coat with hoisin sauce or mustard.
- Spread a sauce (e.g. mayonnaise, pesto, olive and anchovy pastes) over the grilled poultry then pop it back under the grill for a couple of minutes.

Poultry also responds well to cooking 'en papillote'. For ideas see page 144.

——— *Chicken Breast with Lemon Sauce* ———

light, fresh-flavoured dish that nevertheless tastes luxurious.
1en fresh herbs such as basil, marjoram, thyme, chives or
ragon are available, add some to give the dish a summery
vour.

proximately 175ml/6fl oz	1 chicken breast, skinned
hicken stock and medium-	1 small egg yolk
odied dry white wine,	1½ tablespoons lemon juice
nixed	

r the stock and wine into a pan in which the chicken will just
bring to the boil, add the chicken, reduce the heat so the
id barely moves then poach the chicken breast uncovered for
it 12–15 minutes or until tender, turning the breast over
it halfway through. Using a slotted spoon, transfer the
ken to a warmed plate, cover and keep warm.

oil the cooking liquid until reduced by about half. Blend the
yolk with the lemon juice and a little of the cooking liquor,
into the pan and heat very gently, whisking constantly,
thickened – do not allow to boil. (If the sauce does start to
a little grainy, quickly pour it into a blender and give it a
t whizz then pour it back into the pan and continue to cook
y.) Add any juices that have collected on the plate with the
ken. Season to taste, adjust the amount of lemon juice if
ssary and pour over the chicken.

TION
vour the sauce with a pinch of dried thyme or tarragon:
l to the cooking liquor when the chicken breast has been
loved.

Chicken Breast with Soy-Ginger Butter Sauce

The spring onion and ginger provide just the right foil to the smooth, deep richness of the butter and soy sauce, making a sauce that balances beautifully the texture and mild flavour of chicken.

1 chicken breast
white part 2 spring onions, finely chopped
4 tablespoons medium-bodied dry white wine
¼ teaspoon grated fresh root ginger

40g/1½oz unsalted butter, diced
½ teaspoon soy sauce
approximately ¼ teaspoon lemon juice
salt and freshly ground black pepper

Grill or poach the chicken breast until cooked through.

Meanwhile simmer the spring onions, wine and ginger in a small saucepan until only about 1½ tablespoons of liquid remain. Purée the mixture then return to the saucepan over a very low heat and gradually whisk in the butter, making sure each piece is fully incorporated before adding the next. Add the soy sauce and lemon juice and season to taste.

Remove the skin from the chicken, cut the flesh into slices and pour the sauce over.

Chicken with Pesto Stuffing

Italian ingredients provide the inspiration and flavour for one of the tastiest chicken dishes I know. The thigh or drumstick can be prepared in advance and kept covered in the refrigerator, but transfer it to room temperature about 30 minutes before cooking.

1 tablespoon Ricotta cheese or
  low-fat soft cheese
approximately 1 teaspoon
  pesto
freshly ground black pepper
1 chicken thigh or drumstick,
  skinned and boned
1 large slice Parma ham,
  trimmed

good olive oil
approximately 1 tablespoon
  medium-bodied dry white
  wine
a little chicken stock (optional)
fresh basil sprig, if available,
  for garnish

Blend the cheese and pesto together and season with black pepper. Spread on the inside of the boned thigh or drumstick but do not take it too near to the edges. Fold the flesh over, pressing the edges together to seal. Sprinkle a little black pepper over the outside of the chicken then enclose completely in the Parma ham, folding and tucking it under. Heat a little oil in a small, heavy pan, add the chicken and brown quickly on both sides. Add the wine, lower the heat, cover and cook gently for about 20–25 minutes. Use a heat-diffusing mat if necessary and add a little wine, chicken stock or water if the pan becomes dry.

Transfer the chicken to a warmed plate and keep warm. Boil the cooking juices until reduced slightly then spoon over the chicken. Garnish with fresh basil, if available.

Chicken Breast with Broccoli

The green of the sauce next to the white of the chicken flesh makes this dish look as good as it tastes. If the broccoli has stalks, cook them for slightly longer and use in the sauce.

15g/½oz unsalted butter
1 small shallot, finely chopped
3 tablespoons medium-bodied
   dry white wine (optional)
150ml/5fl oz chicken stock
1 chicken breast, skinned

85g/3oz broccoli florets
approximately 2 tablespoons
   Greek yogurt, fromage blanc
   or double cream
salt and freshly ground black
   pepper

Heat the butter in a pan in which the chicken breast will just fit, add the shallot and cook over a low heat until softened but not coloured. Add the wine, if using, and boil until almost completely evaporated. Add the stock, heat to simmering point then add the chicken breast, cover and reduce the heat so the liquid barely moves. Poach gently for about 12–15 minutes or until thoroughly cooked. Remove the chicken from the pan and keep warm. Boil the liquid until reduced to about 4 tablespoons. Meanwhile steam the broccoli for about 3–4 minutes until just tender. Drain then refresh under running water and drain well. Reserve half of the broccoli and keep warm. Purée the remainder in a blender with the yogurt, fromage blanc or cream, and the liquid in which the chicken was cooked and mix until smooth. Pour back into the pan, add any cooking juices that have collected from the chicken breast, and reheat gently. Season to taste. Spoon or pour the sauce over and around the chicken and add the reserved broccoli florets.

VARIATIONS

- As the flavour of lightly toasted flaked almonds goes well with both chicken and broccoli, a few sprinkled over as a garnish has a magical effect. It will also add another dimension to the texture and make the dish look even more attractive.

- If you prefer a more creamy sauce, boil the stock to reduce to about 2 tablespoons after cooking the chicken and increase the amount of yogurt, fromage blanc or cream to 4 tablespoons, or to taste.

- Add a small knob of butter to the sauce when puréeing it.

Chicken with Orange,
Ginger and Yogurt

The chicken benefits most from the tenderizing effect and the flavours of the yogurt marinade if left for 12 hours, but it can be cooked after less time. If you plan to eat it in the evening after a day at work, prepare the yogurt mixture the evening before so that you only have to add the chicken to it in the morning.

2 chicken drumsticks, skinned
2 tablespoons orange juice
pinch grated orange rind
   (optional)
4 tablespoons Greek yogurt
2 teaspoons grated fresh
   ginger

½ clove garlic, crushed, or
   garlic purée to taste
   (optional)
1 teaspoon soy sauce
freshly ground black pepper
sliced spring onions, for
   garnish

Prick the chicken drumsticks all over with a fork and put them in a shallow, non-metallic, ovenproof dish in which they just fit.

Blend together all the remaining ingredients. Pour over the chicken then turn the drumsticks over to coat them evenly. Cover and leave in the refrigerator for 12 hours, turning the chicken occasionally then leave at room temperature for about 30 minutes. Bake at 200°C/400°F/gas mark 6 for about 1 hour or until golden, basting occasionally with the marinade. Sprinkle with sliced spring onions before serving.

Sesame Chicken

Sesame in three different forms combines to make the chicken wonderfully nutty and succulent.

1 tablespoon tahina (sesame
  seed paste)
approximately 1 teaspoon
  finely chopped garlic or
  garlic purée, to taste
2 teaspoons lemon juice
1 teaspoon finely grated
  lemon rind

¼ teaspoon sesame oil
freshly ground black pepper
1 chicken breast, skinned
approximately 1½ tablespoons
  lightly toasted sesame seeds
1 tablespoon sesame oil

Mix the tahina, garlic to taste, lemon juice, lemon rind, sesame
oil and black pepper together in a bowl. Sprinkle a little lemon
juice over the chicken then spread the tahina mixture evenly
all over. Cover and leave for ½–1 hour. Coat the chicken
evenly with sesame seeds and oil then place under a preheated
hot grill until it begins to turn crisp and brown. Reduce the
heat to moderate and continue to grill, occasionally turning the
chicken carefully without piercing the skin, until cooked
throughout.

VARIATION

● Chicken with Sesame and Lemon – marinate the breast
  in 1½ tablespoons lemon juice for 1 hour, turning
  occasionally. Mix 40g/1½oz sesame seeds with the rind of
  ½ lemon. Coat the breast in seasoned flour then beaten egg
  followed by the sesame seeds. Fry in butter until golden and
  crisp.

—————— *Fragrant Citrus Chicken Wings* ——————

Chicken wings are often disregarded, but they do make very
good eating. The only sensible way to eat them is with the fingers
and when you are on your own you can really relax and enjoy
them. Cooked with this lightly spiced, tangy marinade they are

delicious cold as well as hot. Two wings make a first course or a light meal with a salad and crusty bread.

1 clove garlic, crushed
finely grated rind ½ orange
1 tablespoon orange juice
approximately ½ teaspoon
  lime or lemon juice
a few cardamom seeds, toasted
  and crushed
salt and freshly ground black
  pepper
2 chicken wings

Mix the first six ingredients together. Put the chicken wings into a small, shallow, non-metallic, ovenproof dish, pour the marinade over, cover and leave for 4 hours, turning the chicken occasionally.

Bake the wings, uncovered, at 200°C/400°F/gas mark 6 for about 18–20 minutes, basting occasionally, until golden. Eat hot or cold.

Spicy Chicken Wings

Instead of chicken wings you could use 2 largish drumsticks or 1 chicken portion. Slash the chicken several times with the point of a sharp knife to allow the sauce to penetrate the flesh.

1 teaspoon chilli sauce
2 teaspoons Spanish sherry
  vinegar
2 teaspoons finely chopped
  garlic
½ teaspoon soy sauce
1½ teaspoons ground bean
  sauce (available in cans or
  bottles)
3 chicken wings

Mix the chilli sauce with the vinegar, garlic, soy sauce and ground bean sauce. Place the chicken in a small ovenproof dish, pour the sauce over and leave to marinate for an hour or more, turning the chicken over occasionally and basting with the sauce.

Bake the chicken wings in the marinade at 200°C/400°F/gas

mark 6 for about 18–20 minutes or until golden brown and thoroughly cooked.

—————— *Chicken in Spiced Tomato Sauce* ——————

Instead of chicken thighs, drumsticks or a leg portion divided into 2 joints could be used. A heat-diffusing mat may well be necessary.

olive oil
1 shallot, finely chopped
1 small clove garlic, finely
  chopped
1/4 teaspoon ground cumin
1 heaped teaspoon coriander
  seeds, crushed
2 chicken thighs

100ml/3 1/2fl oz passata
  (creamed tomatoes,
  available in cartons)
Tabasco sauce
salt and freshly ground black
  pepper
approximately 1/2 teaspoon
  chopped fresh parsley

Heat a little oil in a nonstick pan just large enough to hold the chicken, add the shallot and garlic and cook, stirring occasionally, until softened but not coloured. Stir in the spices and cook for a minute, still stirring. Scoop out the shallot and garlic and reserve. Add the chicken thighs to the pan and cook, turning them occasionally, until lightly browned. Stir in the tomatoes and add a dash Tabasco sauce and seasoning to taste. Cover tightly and cook over a low heat for about 20 minutes or until the chicken is tender, stirring occasionally. Stir in the parsley and adjust the seasoning if necessary.

————— *Chicken in a Caramelized Cider* ————— *and Apple Sauce*

The lightly caramelized sauce gives a deep, rich flavour to this dish.

5 tablespoons dry cider

1 chicken portion

½ teaspoon finely grated
  lemon rind

salt and freshly ground black
  pepper

unsalted butter and oil

1 small, crisp, tasty eating
  apple, thinly sliced

1 shallot, finely chopped

1½ teaspoons sugar

lemon juice (optional)

Pour the cider over the chicken in a small dish, sprinkle the lemon rind and seasoning over and leave at room temperature for 2 hours, turning the chicken occasionally.

Remove the chicken from the marinade, allowing the excess to drain off, and pat dry. Heat a little butter and oil in a heavy flameproof casserole or saucepan in which the chicken will just fit. Add the chicken and cook until lightly browned on both sides. Take the pan off the heat, remove the chicken then put the apple and shallot in the pan and place the chicken on top.

In a small heavy saucepan, gently heat the sugar in a few drops of water until it dissolves then cook over a moderate heat until it begins to become a rich brown. Remove from the heat and immediately pour the marinade into the pan – take care as it will probably splutter. Return to the heat and cook gently, stirring, until the caramel has dissolved. Pour over the chicken, cover tightly and cook over a very low heat for about 25 minutes, or until tender.

Using a slotted spoon, transfer the chicken and apple to a warmed serving plate. Boil the cooking juices until they begin to thicken. Taste and adjust the seasoning and add a little lemon juice, if necessary. Spoon over the chicken.

VARIATION

- To make more of a sauce, swirl a diced small knob of unsalted butter into the cooking juices before adding the seasoning and lemon juice. Alternatively, use fromage blanc or Greek yogurt, just leave on the heat long enough for the sauce to warm through then season.

Chicken Pot-roasted with Rosemary and Garlic

The simplest of ways to cook chicken so that it remains moist and is delicately flavoured.

15g/½oz unsalted butter
1 tablespoon olive oil
1 clove garlic, roughly crushed
1 chicken joint
small rosemary sprig, broken

in half, or small pinch dried rosemary
salt and freshly ground black pepper
2 tablespoons medium-bodied dry white wine

Heat the butter and oil together in a small, heavy flameproof pan over a moderately high heat. Add the garlic and chicken and cook until the chicken is evenly browned. Turn the chicken over and add the rosemary, seasoning and wine. Allow the wine to bubble for 2 minutes then lower the heat, cover the pan tightly and leave the chicken to cook slowly until tender. Use a heat-diffusing mat if necessary.

Transfer the chicken to a warmed plate. Discard the pieces of fresh rosemary, if using, and spoon off the fat from the cooking juices, unless you like it. Spoon the fat-free juices over the chicken.

Wine- and Honey-glazed Chicken

If the chicken is left in the refrigerator during the day, allow it to come to room temperature for 30 minutes before cooking. The cool tang of the lime juice squeezed over the chicken contrasts with the hot, sweet honey.

3–4 chicken wings or 2 chicken drumsticks

2 teaspoons olive oil

2 teaspoons medium-bodied dry white wine

1½ tablespoons lime juice

2 teaspoons clear honey

1 teaspoon each chopped fresh parsley and marjoram or thyme

salt and freshly ground black pepper

lime wedges, to serve

Place the wings or drumsticks in an oiled ovenproof dish. Mix the olive oil, wine, lime juice and honey together until the honey has dissolved then add the herbs, salt and pepper. Pour over the chicken, cover and leave in a cool place for at least 4 hours, turning frequently.

Bake the chicken, uncovered, for 30–40 minutes at 190°C/375°F/gas mark 5, basting frequently, until the chicken is tender and golden – keep an eye on it to make sure the honey does not burn. Alternatively, cook on the lowest rack under a moderate grill, basting and turning frequently, for about 25 minutes or until tender and golden.

Transfer the chicken to a warmed serving plate and serve with lime wedges to squeeze over.

Poached Poussin with a Hint of North African Spices

Poaching the poussin makes the flesh meltingly tender, and the spices add a delicate, exotic flavour. It is also very good cold – leave the bird to cool in the liquor.

30g/1oz couscous

small pinch ground cinnamon

very small pinch ground
  cloves

1/4 teaspoon orange flower
  water

salt and freshly ground black
  pepper

1 1/2 teaspoons sugar

1 tablespoon raisins

1 tablespoon chopped almonds

1 fresh poussin

1 shallot, finely chopped

1/4 teaspoon grated fresh root
  ginger

approximately 3cm/1 1/4in
  piece cinnamon

1/2 teaspoon mild honey

Stir into the couscous a little less than its volume of water, leave
for 5 minutes then add the ground cinnamon, cloves, orange
flower water, seasoning and sugar. Stir in the raisins and almonds
and spoon a small amount into the cavity of the poussin.

Pour 150ml/1/4 pint water into a saucepan just large enough to
hold the poussin then add the shallot, ginger, cinnamon stick
and a little seasoning. Bring to simmering point, add the poussin,
cover and poach gently for about 25 minutes, turning the bird
over two or three times. Add the honey and cook for another 10
minutes or so, until tender.

Meanwhile, warm the remaining couscous in a small bowl
placed over a saucepan of simmering water.

Remove the poussin and cinnamon from the pan, place the
poussin on a warmed plate and spoon the couscous in the cavity to
one side, with the remaining couscous. Keep warm. Boil the cooking
juices until reduced then pour over the poussin and couscous.

VARIATION
- Substitute a chicken portion for the poussin, and reduce the
  cooking time to 20 minutes.

— *Poussin with Grapes* —

Although the length of the method makes it appear to be
complicated, this is in fact a very simple, light dish.

175g/6oz seedless Muscat
grapes, halved
1 fresh poussin
salt and freshly ground black
pepper

2 tablespoons medium-bodied
dry white wine (optional)
1 tablespoon Greek yogurt
lemon juice (optional)

Reserve 4 grape halves. Put about 6 grape halves into the poussin cavity then season the bird inside and out.

Fry the poussin in a nonstick pan until it is a light golden brown all over.

Put most of the grapes on a piece of foil large enough to wrap round the poussin. Place the poussin on the grapes then put the remaining grapes on the poussin. Fold the sides of the foil up.

Stir the wine, if using, or 2 tablespoons water into the pan to dislodge the sediment then bring to the boil. Leave to bubble for 2 minutes then pour over the poussin. Fold the foil completely over the bird, sealing the edges tightly together. Place in a steaming basket or colander, cover the basket or colander, and place over a saucepan of boiling water. Steam for 25 minutes or until thoroughly cooked.

Unwrap the poussin, transfer to a warmed plate and keep warm. Purée the grapes with the cooking juices then boil in a small pan until reduced to about 5 tablespoonfuls. Add any juices that have collected on the plate with the poussin. Lower the heat and stir in the yogurt – do not allow to boil. Adjust the seasoning and add a little lemon juice, if necessary, to lift the flavour.

Remove the grapes from the poussin cavity and place next to the poussin then pour the sauce over the bird. Scatter the reserved grape halves over.

VARIATION
- If Muscat grapes are not available, use another variety with a good flavour and sprinkle 2–3 drops orange flower water on them, except the ones placed in the cavity and the ones reserved for garnish. Adjust the level of orange flower water when tasting for seasoning.

————— *Turkey with Lemon and Capers* —————

A simple, clean, fresh-tasting dish that is cooked in a matter of minutes.

unsalted butter
1 turkey escalope
salt and freshly ground black
  pepper
approximately 1 tablespoon
  lemon juice

approximately 2 teaspoons
  roughly chopped capers
finely chopped fresh parsley
  and a lemon wedge, to serve

Heat about 15g/½oz butter in a pan, add the turkey and cook lightly on both sides until just cooked through but barely coloured on the outside. Transfer to a warmed serving plate, season sparingly and keep warm.

Stir the lemon juice into the cooking juices, dislodging any sediment and adding a teaspoon or so of water if necessary. Bring to the boil briefly, stir in a little more butter, the capers and any juices that have collected on the plate with the turkey.

Pour the sauce over the turkey, sprinkle a little parsley over and serve with a lemon wedge.

VARIATIONS
● Use 1 scant teaspoon crushed black peppercorns instead of the capers.
● Use a veal escalope instead of turkey.

Turkey with Tomatoes and Olives

olive oil
1 shallot, finely chopped
1 clove garlic, crushed
2 medium–large full-flavoured
   tomatoes, skinned, seeds
   removed, chopped
4 black olives, stoned and
   quartered
small pinch oregano
salt and freshly ground black
   pepper
1 turkey escalope

Heat a little oil in a small pan, add the shallot and cook, stirring occasionally, until softened and beginning to colour. Add the garlic, cook until coloured slightly then stir in the tomatoes. Allow the mixture to simmer quite briskly until it starts to thicken, stirring quite frequently as it gets thicker. Add the olives and oregano and season to taste – only a very little salt will be needed because of the saltiness of the olives.

In a separate pan quickly fry the turkey in hot oil until lightly browned and thoroughly cooked. Season lightly and transfer to a warmed plate. Pour the sauce over.

VARIATION
● The sauce also goes well with chicken, grilled poussin, or duck leg or breast.

Turkey with Quick Creamy Tomato and Herb Sauce

Soft cheeses are very useful for making creamy-tasting dishes without cream. The higher the fat content of the cheese, the richer-tasting the dish but, obviously, the higher the number of calories.

1 turkey escalope or steak
white part 1 spring onion,
    finely chopped
2 tablespoons plain yogurt
1 scant teaspoon tomato purée
1½ teaspoons dry white
    vermouth (optional)

30g/1oz full-fat soft cheese
approximately 3 fresh basil
    leaves, or pinch dried
    tarragon
salt and freshly ground black
    pepper

Grill or fry the turkey. Meanwhile in a small saucepan gently simmer the spring onion (with the dried tarragon, if using) in about 1 tablespoon water for 2 minutes. Mix the yogurt, tomato purée and vermouth, if using, with the cheese then stir into the saucepan and heat through. If using basil, tear the leaves into pieces and add to the sauce. Add seasoning to taste, and add a little more water to the sauce, if necessary, to get a fairly thick consistency. Pour over the turkey.

Turkey with Yellow Bean Sauce

The Chinese flavours of the marinade make an unusual combination with turkey and give it a new succulence and taste.

1 tablespoon yellow bean
    sauce
1 tablespoon dark soy sauce
½ tablespoon rice wine or dry
    sherry
½ teaspoon fresh green chilli,

seeded and cut into fine
    rings, or chilli or Tabasco
    sauce
approximately 150g/5oz
    turkey, cut into thick strips
oil

Mix the first four ingredients together in a shallow dish. Add the turkey, stir to coat, cover and leave for 1–2 hours.

Heat a little oil in a nonstick pan. Remove the turkey from the marinade, add to the pan and fry over a fairly high heat, stirring, for 2 minutes, until almost cooked. Stir in the marinade and continue to cook until the sauce has reduced and the meat is well-coated and moist.

Duck with Anchovy Sauce

The combination of anchovy and duck is well known but in no recipe is it more successful than this one, in which the sharpness of lemon and the saltiness of anchovies in the sauce make a perfect contrast to the richness of the duck. A simple crisp salad goes well with it.

1 teaspoon anchovy paste or purée
1 teaspoon lemon juice
1 teaspoon grated lemon rind
15g/½oz unsalted butter
1 tablespoon virgin olive oil
freshly ground black pepper
1 duck breast
salt

In a small bowl mix together the anchovy paste or purée, lemon juice and rind, butter and oil. Add black pepper to taste.

With the point of a sharp knife, slash the duck skin in three places. Rub salt into the skin then sprinkle black pepper over.

Cook the breast skin-side uppermost under a hot grill for about 4 minutes. Turn the breast over, turn the heat down a little and continue to cook for 4–5 minutes or until just pink in the centre.

Leave the duck to rest, covered, in a warm place for 5 minutes. Remove the skin, if wished, cut the breast into slices and spoon the sauce over.

Caramelized Duck and Orange

This is a dish for when you really care about what you are going to eat – not because it is difficult but because it has the feel of a treat. It is complemented by a crisp salad of curly endive, or one containing watercress or fresh coriander, and orange segments.

1 duck breast
approximately 1 teaspoon
  finely chopped root ginger
salt and freshly ground black
  pepper
finely grated rind ½ orange
3 tablespoons orange juice

1 teaspoon sugar
2½ teaspoons white wine
  vinegar
115ml/4fl oz chicken stock
3 tablespoons double cream
approximately 1 tablespoon
  toasted flaked almonds

Carefully loosen the duck skin from the flesh and slip in the ginger, distributing it evenly. Lay the skin back in place and season the outside of the skin.

Place the duck skin-side uppermost under a hot grill and cook for 2–3 minutes until the skin becomes crisp then turn the duck over, without piercing the flesh, and cook for 2 minutes. Lower the heat slightly and continue to cook for 4–5 minutes, depending on how well done you like it. While the duck is cooking, simmer the orange rind, juice and sugar in a small heavy saucepan until it begins to look slightly caramelized. Remove from the heat, stir in the vinegar then return to the heat and cook until the caramel has dissolved and the liquid reduced slightly. Stir in the stock and simmer until reduced by about half. Stir in the cream and cook over a very low heat for about 10 minutes. Season to taste. Pour the sauce around the duck on a warmed serving plate and sprinkle with toasted flaked almonds.

VARIATIONS
- For a less rich sauce substitute fromage blanc or Greek yogurt for the cream.
- Lightly toasted sliced hazelnuts can be used instead of almonds.
- Add a garnish of orange segments, if you have the time and inclination to remove all the pith and skin.

Duck Breast with Passion Fruit Sauce

1 passion fruit
1 duck breast
3 tablespoons medium-bodied
   dry white wine

salt and freshly ground white
   pepper

Squeeze the juice from the passion fruit, reserving the seeds. Pour the juice on to the duck in a small dish and spread the seeds over the surface. Cover and leave in a cool place for 3 hours.

Preheat the grill to very high. Remove the duck from the marinade and brush off any seeds adhering to it; reserve the marinade and seeds. Place the duck close to the grill to lightly char the surface on one side then move it slightly lower down to cook through a little more for about 2½–3 minutes per side, but leave pink in the centre.

Meanwhile, boil the wine in a small saucepan until reduced to about 1 tablespoon then stir in the reserved juice and seeds and season to taste. Serve the duck with the sauce spooned over.

VARIATION
● Omit the wine and simply pour the reserved juice and seeds over the cooked duck.

Quails Braised with Red Cabbage and Juniper

Quails are good for solo eating – they cook quickly but take some time to eat because they are a little fiddly, which makes the meal last longer; one of the drawbacks of eating alone is the speed with which meals tend to be finished. Also, because they are fiddly, quails might be something that you would avoid eating in company.

Cooking with red cabbage and juniper makes this dish seem quite 'gamey'.

1 small rasher bacon, chopped
olive oil
1 shallot, chopped
2 small thyme sprigs
(optional)
2 quails
½ small red cabbage (about
115–150g/4–5oz), thinly
sliced
3 juniper berries, lightly
crushed

approximately 3 tablespoons
red wine, or chicken, veal or
vegetable stock
salt and freshly ground black
pepper
approximately 2 tablespoons
raisins, or 4 prunes, stoned,
or 1 tablespoon redcurrant
jelly

In a heavy, flameproof casserole in which the cabbage and quails will fit snugly, fry the bacon in a little oil until it becomes crisp then add the shallot and cook for about 3 minutes. Place a sprig of thyme, if using, inside each quail then add the birds to the pan and quickly brown on all sides. Remove the quails and keep warm. Stir the cabbage and juniper berries into the pan and cook for about 3 minutes, stirring occasionally then pour in the wine or stock and bring to the boil. Season, add the raisins or prunes, if using, and place the quails on top. Cover tightly and cook slowly until the quails are tender – about 35–40 minutes. If using redcurrant jelly, lift out the quails when they are cooked and stir in the jelly, to taste.

VARIATIONS
● Place a piece of spicy garlic sausage inside each bird.
● Substitute 1 pigeon for the quails, and cook for about an hour – pigeons can vary quite considerably in their toughness, depending on whether they are farmed or wild and, if the latter, their age.

MEAT

Grilled Meats

There are many ways of livening up grilled meats, for example:
- Brushing or basting with oil flavoured with fresh or dried herbs, such as rosemary, fennel, thyme, tarragon, basil, chives, marjoram and oregano.
- Marinating in oil and lemon juice flavoured with herbs, or with paprika or other spices, such as Chinese five-spice powder (for notes on marinating see page 164).
- Coating with hoisin sauce or mustard.
- Spreading a sauce (e.g. mayonnaise, pesto, olive and anchovy pastes) over the grilled meat, then putting it back under the grill for a couple of minutes.

Lamb with Peas and Lettuce

small knob butter
2 lamb cutlets or 1 lamb steak
1–2 tablespoons medium-
  bodied dry white wine
  (optional)
85g/3oz thawed frozen peas
1 large or 2 small spring
  onions, chopped

1 large lettuce leaf or 2–3
  smaller ones, shredded
1 teaspoon finely chopped
  fresh parsley
salt and freshly ground black
  pepper

Heat most of the butter in a saucepan, add the lamb and cook over a moderately high heat until lightly browned on both sides. Transfer to absorbent kitchen paper to drain. Stir the wine, if using (otherwise substitute water), into the cooking juices and bring to the boil, stirring. Lower the heat then stir in the peas, spring onion, lettuce, parsley and seasoning, coating the vegetables with the liquid. Place the lamb on top, cover the pan and cook over a very low heat for about 25 minutes or until the meat is just tender and pink inside.

Transfer the lamb to a warmed plate. If there is too much liquid in the pan increase the heat and boil off most of it. Return to the pan any cooking juices that have collected on the plate with the lamb and add the remaining butter. Taste and adjust the seasoning then pour around the lamb.

VARIATION
● Add 1 tablespoon double cream, Greek yogurt or fromage blanc instead of butter at the end of the cooking. If using cream, boil until lightly thickened; if using yogurt or fromage blanc just warm through gently.

Lamb with Flageolet Sauce

15g/½oz unsalted butter or 1 tablespoon olive oil
2 lamb cutlets
1 small leek, thinly sliced
1 small clove garlic, crushed
115g/4oz cooked flageolet beans, or rinsed canned ones
salt and freshly ground black pepper
1 tablespoon medium-bodied dry white wine (optional)
1 teaspoon tarragon mustard

Heat the butter or oil in a pan, add the lamb cutlets and brown on both sides then transfer to absorbent paper to drain. Add the leek and garlic to the pan and cook, stirring occasionally, for 2–3 minutes. Stir in the flageolet beans, seasoning, wine, if using, and mustard. Bring to the boil, place the lamb on top, lower the heat, cover the pan and cook gently until the lamb is tender and still pink in the centre – about 20 minutes.

Using a slotted spoon, transfer the lamb and some of the beans to a warmed plate and keep warm. Purée the remaining contents of the pan then return to the pan, bring to the boil and, if necessary, simmer, stirring frequently, until lightly thickened. Adjust the seasoning and mustard to taste.

Spoon on to a serving plate, put the lamb on top and scatter the reserved beans over.

Lamb with Five-spice Redcurrant Sauce

I am not a lover of plain redcurrant jelly with lamb or, for that matter, other sweet jellies with meat, although I know many people are. But redcurrant jelly sharpened with orange and lime or lemon juice and given a lift by five-spice powder really does add something to the lamb – and to venison as well.

freshly ground black pepper
1 lamb steak or 2 cutlets
1½ tablespoons redcurrant
  jelly
1½ tablespoons orange juice

scant ¼ teaspoon Chinese
  five-spice powder
very small knob unsalted
  butter (optional)
salt
lime or lemon juice

Grind black pepper over the lamb then either grill or fry until tender but still pink in the centre.

Meanwhile melt the redcurrant jelly in a small heavy saucepan with the orange juice and five-spice powder, stirring. Bring to the boil and boil until slightly syrupy – about 3 minutes. Swirl in a small knob of butter, if liked, and add seasoning and lime or lemon juice to taste. Serve with the lamb.

Aromatic Lamb Steak

This is good served with a sauce of Greek yogurt mixed with finely chopped fresh coriander.

1 teaspoon wholegrain
  mustard
¼ teaspoon finely crushed
  cumin seeds
½ teaspoon finely crushed
  coriander seeds

2 teaspoons lemon or lime
  juice
1 teaspoon tahina
1 small clove garlic, finely
  chopped
1 lamb steak

In a small bowl, stir the mustard, cumin and coriander seeds, lemon or lime juice, tahina and garlic together. Spread over the lamb, cover and leave at a cool room temperature for up to 2 hours. Alternatively leave in the fridge for up to 8 hours but return to room temperature about 30 minutes before cooking.

Cook the lamb under a preheated hot grill for 3–4 minutes each side.

Spicy Lemon Lamb

1½ tablespoons lemon juice
¼ teaspoon ground coriander
¼ teaspoon ground cumin
¼ teaspoon garlic purée

approximately 175g/6oz lean
  lamb, cubed
bay leaves, preferably fresh
salt and freshly ground black
  pepper

Mix the lemon juice, spices and garlic purée together in a dish. Add the lamb, turning to coat in the mixture then leave to marinate at room temperature for up to 2 hours, turning the lamb frequently.

Thread the lamb on to one or two skewers, alternating with fresh bay leaves. Cook under a preheated hot grill for 6–7 minutes, turning frequently to ensure even cooking and brushing with marinade, until the lamb is tender.

Pour any remaining marinade into a small saucepan and heat through. Add a little salt and pepper, and a little more lemon juice if necessary, and spoon over the kebabs.

VARIATION
● Vegetables, such as cooked, unpeeled, small new potatoes, chunks of courgette or mushrooms, can be alternated with the cubes of lamb on the skewers.

Grilled Lamb with Lemon and Mixed Herbs

The longer the lamb is left to marinate, the more tender it will become and the quicker it will cook. The combination of herbs can be varied according to what is available.

½ teaspoon each finely
   chopped fresh rosemary,
   marjoram, chives and
   parsley
1 tablespoon olive oil

3 tablespoons lemon juice
1 lamb steak
salt and freshly ground black
   pepper

Mix the herbs, oil and lemon juice together. Lay the lamb in a small, shallow, non-metallic dish, pour the marinade over, cover and leave in the refrigerator for 1–8 hours, turning the lamb over in the marinade occasionally.

Remove the lamb from the marinade, allowing the excess to drain off then cook under a preheated hot grill for 6–8 minutes, turning over halfway through. Serve with any remaining marinade spooned over.

—— Lamb with Spiced Hoisin Sauce ——

pinch finely crushed toasted
   Sichuan peppercorns
small pinch cayenne pepper

small pinch ground cumin
2 teaspoons hoisin sauce
1 lamb steak

Mix the spices together then stir in the hoisin sauce. Spread over the lamb, place on a grill rack and leave for about an hour.

Place the grill rack under a preheated hot grill and cook the lamb for about 3–4 minutes a side until evenly browned on the outside but still just pink and moist on the inside.

VARIATION
● Use pork, chicken or turkey instead of lamb.

—— Lamb with Orange and Aniseed ——

Cooking lamb slowly in an orange and aniseed sauce gives it an enticing, spicy, pungent, warming flavour. If you do not want to heat up the oven, or if you do not have one, it can be cooked in a small heavy saucepan or flameproof casserole into which the lamb will just fit. Make sure the pan is tightly covered and place it over a very low heat; reduce the cooking time by about 5–10 minutes.

1 lamb steak or 2 lamb cutlets	1 ½ teaspoons soft brown sugar or honey
115ml/4fl oz orange juice	
1 scant teaspoon aniseed, crushed	salt and freshly ground black pepper
0.5cm/¼in piece fresh root ginger, peeled and grated (optional)	1 ½ teaspoons dry sherry (optional)
	orange slices, for garnish

Put the lamb in a small, non-metallic ovenproof dish. Mix the orange juice, aniseed, ginger, if using, sugar or honey, and seasoning together. Pour over the lamb and leave at room temperature for 1 hour.

Cover the dish and bake at 170°C/325°F/gas mark 3 for about 35–40 minutes, or until as tender as you like casseroled lamb to be. Baste it frequently.

Use a slotted spoon to transfer the lamb to a warmed serving plate; cover and keep warm. Pour the cooking liquid into a small saucepan, skim the fat from the surface, add the sherry, if using then boil until lightly thickened. Taste and adjust the seasoning then pour over the lamb. Garnish with orange slices.

VARIATIONS
- Substitute pork or chicken for the lamb.
- Whisk a small nut of butter into the reduced sauce to give it a richer sheen and flavour.

Lamb with Orange and Nuts

olive oil
white part 2 spring onions,
   chopped
approximately 150g/5oz lamb
   steak or lean lamb, cut into
   cubes

1 tablespoon cashew or other
   nuts
1 tablespoon dry sherry
grated orange rind
salt and freshly ground black
   pepper

Heat a little oil in a pan, add the spring onions and cook until softened. Stir in the lamb and nuts and cook, stirring, for about 3−4 minutes, until the lamb is browned but still pink on the inside. Stir in the sherry, bubble to evaporate off some of the liquid then add a little grated orange rind and seasoning to taste.

VARIATION
● Use 3 tablespoons medium-bodied dry white wine instead of the sherry.

Veal with Lemon and Parsley

A garnish that adds to the flavour as well as the appearance can be made by cutting the rind of ½ small lemon into fine strips, bringing it to the boil in some water in a small saucepan over a moderate heat, draining, refreshing under cold running water then draining again. Return the rind to the saucepan, add a very small pinch of sugar and 2 teaspoons water and heat again, over a low heat, until the water has just evaporated.

unsalted butter
olive oil
1 slice veal fillet, about 150g/
5oz
3 tablespoons medium-bodied
dry white wine (optional)

approximately 1 tablespoon
lemon juice
½–1 tablespoon chopped fresh
parsley
salt and freshly ground white
pepper
lemon wedge, to serve

Heat a small knob of butter and a little olive oil in a small nonstick frying pan, add the veal and cook over a moderate heat until lightly browned on both sides. Transfer the veal to a warmed plate, cover and keep warm. Stir the wine, if using (or substitute water), into the pan, dislodging the sediment, and boil until reduced to about 1½ teaspoons. Add the lemon juice then, over a low heat, gradually but quickly whisk in a small knob of butter. Pour in any veal juices that have collected on the plate then add the parsley and seasoning.

Add the veal, turn it over in the sauce then transfer to a warmed plate and place a lemon wedge beside it.

Pork with Chinese Five-spice Powder

Use the back of a teaspoon to spread the spice mixture over the pork. A crisp green salad, or lightly fried strips of red pepper, mangetout and spring onions, makes a good accompaniment.

½ teaspoon Chinese five-spice
powder
freshly ground black pepper

½ teaspoon sesame oil
lime juice
1 boneless pork chop

Blend the five-spice powder, black pepper and oil together. Sprinkle lime juice over the chop then spread evenly with the spice mixture. Leave at room temperature for 30–60 minutes.

Cook the chop under a preheated moderate to moderately hot grill for about 4–5 minutes per side until brown on the outside and just cooked through but still moist in the centre.

— *Pork with Black Bean Sauce* —

approximately 150g/5oz pork
  steak, cut into thin slices
1 teaspoon rice wine or dry
  sherry
1 teaspoon light soy sauce
groundnut oil

2 teaspoons coarsely chopped
  black beans (available in
  cans)
½ small clove garlic, finely
  chopped
1 fat spring onion bulb, finely
  chopped

Put the pork into a bowl. Mix the rice wine or sherry with the soy sauce, pour over the pork, cover and leave for 30–60 minutes.

Heat a little groundnut oil in a small nonstick pan. Remove the pork from the marinade, add to the hot oil, and cook for about 1½ minutes on each side. Add the black beans, garlic and any remaining marinade and bring to the boil then serve with the spring onion scattered over.

VARIATION
● Add a little grated fresh root ginger to the marinade.

— *Pork Fillet with Mushrooms* —

If you are able to find only whole pieces of pork fillet, also called tenderloin, which weigh about 350g/12oz, double the recipe and keep the second portion for another day. My favourite

accompaniments for this richly flavoured dish are noodles, courgettes and red pepper, or a salad.

oil

115–175g/4–6oz pork fillet

1 shallot or small onion, finely
  chopped

85g/3oz shiitake, oyster or
  brown mushrooms, or
  button mushrooms,
  chopped

4 tablespoons medium-bodied
  dry white wine

approximately ½ teaspoon
  tomato purée

approximately ¼–½ teaspoon
  wholegrain or Dijon
  mustard

salt and freshly ground black
  pepper

Heat a little oil in a saucepan and cook the pork slowly, turning
it occasionally, until almost tender. Add the shallot or onion and
the mushrooms and cook, stirring occasionally, for 2 minutes.
Remove the pork, place on a warmed plate, cover and keep
warm.

Mix the wine with the tomato purée then pour into the pan,
stirring. Bubble for 2 minutes to reduce the liquid then add the
mustard and seasoning and adjust the balance of the other
flavourings.

Cut the pork into slices and serve with the sauce poured
around.

—————— *Pork with Pear and Sage* ——————

Use the remaining pear half in another recipe, such as Cinnamon
Pear Bun (see page 226) or Pear Vinaigrette (see page 236).

unsalted butter
2 slices boneless pork loin,
    about 70g/2½oz each
½ large ripe pear, cored and
    cut into thick slices

approximately 3 sage leaves,
    shredded
2 tablespoons medium-bodied
    dry white wine
salt and freshly ground black
    pepper

Heat a little butter in a frying pan, add the pork slices and cook for
2 minutes. Turn them over, add the pear and sage and cook for a
further 2 minutes. Turn the slices of pear over and cook for another
couple of minutes, but take care not to overcook them. Add the
wine and bubble gently until slightly reduced.

Transfer the pork and pear to a warmed plate, adjust the
seasoning of the sauce and spoon over the pork.

VARIATIONS
● Substitute cider or apple juice for the wine. If you use apple
  juice it may be necessary to lift the sauce with a little lemon
  juice.
● Substitute apple for the pear.
● Finish the sauce by stirring in a little cream or whisking in a
  little unsalted butter.

Pork with Cucumber and Chervil Sauce

The cool crispness of cucumber complements pork very well.

approximately 5cm/2in piece of cucumber, seeds removed if necessary, cut into matchsticks
salt
olive oil
approximately 115g/4oz lean pork, cut into strips

1–2 tablespoons medium-bodied dry white wine
2 tablespoons Greek yogurt
approximately 1 tablespoon chopped fresh chervil
freshly ground black pepper
chervil sprigs, for garnish

Sprinkle the cucumber pieces with salt, place in a colander and leave to drain for 20 minutes. Rinse then dry with absorbent kitchen paper.

Heat a little oil in a nonstick pan, add the pork strips and cook, stirring, for 3–4 minutes. Stir in the cucumber and cook, stirring, for 2 minutes. Add the wine, bubble for a couple of minutes or so then stir in the yogurt and chervil and heat through, but do not allow to boil. Season to taste and serve garnished with sprigs of chervil.

Pork and Apple Skewers

Serve with a crisp salad that includes watercress.

1 small, crisp apple
approximately 175g/6oz lean
   pork, cut into bite-sized
   pieces
lemon juice
1 tablespoon apple juice
½ teaspoon sesame oil

salt and freshly ground black
   pepper
1½ teaspoons toasted sesame
   seeds
fresh coriander sprigs, for
   garnish

Core the apple, cut into quarters then cut each quarter horizontally into 3 or 4 pieces. Mix with the pork in a small bowl and sprinkle a little lemon juice over.

Mix the apple juice, sesame oil and seasoning together. Pour over the pork and apple, stir to mix evenly then leave to marinate for about half an hour.

Use a slotted spoon to remove the pork and apple from the marinade, allowing the excess to drain off. Pat dry then thread alternately on to skewers. Place under a moderately hot grill for about 8 minutes, turning frequently and basting with the marinade.

Roll the pork and apple skewers in the sesame seeds to coat then serve garnished with fresh coriander.

Grilled Steaks with Grilled Radicchio

1 steak
olive oil or melted butter
   (optional)

salt and freshly ground black
   pepper
1 small head radicchio

Brush the steak with olive oil or melted butter, place under a preheated grill and cook for about 3 minutes a side, depending on the type of steak and how well done you like it. Transfer to a warmed plate, season and keep warm.

Reduce the temperature of the grill. Cut the radicchio in half or quarters, depending on its size. Place in an ovenproof dish, spoon olive oil over and sprinkle with a little salt and plenty of freshly ground black pepper. Leave for about 1 minute, turn the pieces of radicchio over in the oil then place briefly under the preheated low grill until softened and beginning to colour a little, or, if you prefer, leave for a little longer, turning the pieces over so they do not burn. Transfer to the same plate as the steak and serve with the cooking juices spooned over.

—————— Steak with Mixed Mushrooms ——————

The various types of mushrooms now being cultivated have a better flavour than ordinary white ones and make dishes much more distinctive. If you can get them, include some wild mushrooms, such as chanterelles and ceps, which are in season throughout the autumn, or morels, which are found in the spring.

selection of salad leaves –
  radicchio, oakleaf, frisé,
  watercress
olive oil and unsalted butter
115g/4oz steak, cut into strips
  or cubes
115g/4oz assorted mushrooms
  – brown cap (chestnut),
  oyster, shiitake

2 tablespoons chopped fresh
  parsley
1 spring onion, chopped
1 tablespoon Spanish sherry
  vinegar
1 tablespoon hazelnut oil
salt and freshly ground black
  pepper

Arrange the salad leaves on a plate.

Heat a little olive oil and butter in a frying pan, add the steak and cook over a fairly high heat for 2–3 minutes, stirring occasionally, until browned on the outside but still pink in the centre. Add the mushrooms and cook for a further 5 minutes. Stir in the parsley, spring onion, sherry vinegar, hazelnut oil and seasoning. Spoon on to the salad leaves.

—— *Steak with Grilled Tomato Sauce* ——

2 medium-sized tomatoes
1 steak
olive oil

salt and freshly ground black
  pepper
1 shallot, finely chopped

Put the grill rack in the lowest position and line the grill pan with foil. Grill the tomatoes, turning them frequently, until the skins blister and become lightly charred. Remove any patches of skin that are hard and black, but no more. Roughly purée the tomatoes, leaving a slight texture. Increase the temperature of the grill and move the grill pan up.

Brush the steak with a little oil then place under the preheated grill for about 3 minutes a side, or until cooked to your liking. Transfer to a warmed plate, season, cover and keep warm.

Heat a little oil in a small pan, add the shallot and cook gently until softened and transparent. Add the tomatoes and cook over a moderate heat until any excess moisture has evaporated and the mixture has thickened slightly. Add the juices that collect on the plate with the steak. Season to taste then pour over or around the steak.

Steak with Roasted
Red Pepper Sauce

1 steak	2 tablespoons crème fraîche,
freshly ground black pepper	fromage blanc or Greek
olive oil	yogurt
1 small red pepper, roasted,	salt
peeled and roughly chopped	

Season both sides of the steak with black pepper then fry in a little hot oil in a heavy frying pan until cooked to your liking. Transfer to a warmed plate and keep warm.

Purée the red pepper then stir in the crème fraîche, fromage blanc or yogurt. Pour into the pan, scraping to dislodge the sediment, and heat gently, stirring. Do not allow to boil. Season with salt and a little black pepper.

Serve the sauce with the steak; the way to do this for the best overall flavour and appearance is to slice the steak at an angle, arrange the slices, overlapping, on a plate then spoon the sauce down the centre of the slices.

VARIATIONS

- If you prefer to grill rather than fry the steak, simply heat the sauce gently in a small saucepan.
- To make a sauce with greater depth of flavour, stir about 3 tablespoons veal stock or wine into the frying pan, scraping to dislodge the sediment, add the chopped red pepper, simmer for 2–3 minutes until the liquid is reduced then purée and season to taste. There is no need to add cream, fromage blanc or yogurt.

The next three recipes are simple ones for using the cooking juices left in the pan after frying steak to make a sauce that enhances the meat. If you prefer less butter reduce the amount and adjust the quantities of other ingredients to taste, if necessary. Use whichever type of steak you prefer — fillet, sirloin or entrecôte, and cook to the degree you like. The recipes can also be made with lamb.

Steak with Shallot Sauce

approximately 40g/1½oz
   unsalted butter
1 steak
1 small shallot, finely chopped
1½ tablespoons sherry vinegar

2 teaspoons chopped fresh
   parsley
salt and freshly ground black
   pepper

Heat about 15g/½oz butter in a small, heavy nonstick frying pan, add the steak and cook for about 3 minutes a side, or until just cooked to the degree you like — it will cook a little more while standing. Transfer the meat to a warmed plate and keep warm.

   Heat the remaining butter in the pan, add the shallot and cook, stirring frequently, until softened but not coloured. Stir in the vinegar and any juices that have collected on the plate with the steak. Boil until reduced by half then add the parsley and season to taste.

   Pour the sauce over the steak.

Steak with Wine Sauce

By using different wines, such as claret or cabernet sauvignon, a burgundy, chianti, barolo, or even a medium- or full-bodied white wine, markedly different sauces can be made.

approximately 40g/1½oz
  unsalted butter
1 steak
1 small shallot, finely chopped
2½ tablespoons wine
½ clove garlic, finely crushed

½ teaspoon chopped fresh
  thyme, tarragon or parsley
approximately ¼ teaspoon
  Dijon mustard
salt and freshly ground black
  pepper

Heat about 15g/½oz butter in a small, heavy nonstick frying pan, add the steak and cook for about 3 minutes a side, or until just cooked to the degree you like – it will cook a little more while standing. Transfer the meat to a warmed plate and keep warm.

Add about ½ teaspoon of the remaining butter to the pan, add the shallot and cook over a fairly high heat for 2 minutes. Stir in the wine, garlic and herb and boil rapidly until about 1½ tablespoons liquid remain. Remove the pan from the heat and gradually whisk in the remaining butter. Add any juices that have collected on the plate with the steak then add mustard and seasoning to taste. Pour the sauce over the steak.

Steak with Anchovy, Lemon and Parsley Sauce

This sauce is extremely simple but very effective with the beef. Although it is better when parsley is added, it is not absolutely essential.

approximately 45g/1½oz
  unsalted butter
2 small garlic clove, finely
  chopped
1 steak
1 anchovy fillet, soaked in
  water or milk and drained

1 teaspoon finely chopped
  fresh parsley
approximately 1 tablespoon
  lemon juice
freshly ground black pepper

Heat about 15g/½oz butter in a small heavy nonstick frying pan, add the garlic and cook, stirring, for 1–2 minutes. Add the steak and brown quickly on both sides. Reduce the heat slightly and cook for a further 1–3 minutes until cooked the way you like it. Transfer the steak to a warmed plate and keep warm.

Add the remaining butter to the pan then stir in the anchovy, mashing it with a wooden spoon, until it dissolves. Stir in the parsley, lemon juice and any juices that have collected on the plate with the steak. Bring to the boil and season with freshly ground black pepper to taste. Pour the sauce over the steak.

Beef with Paprika and Soured Cream

I love the warm, creamy spiciness of this dish. It tastes luxurious and rich, yet is not heavy. I prefer to add the red pepper, but do sometimes make the dish without it.

unsalted butter
1 small onion, chopped
approximately 150g/5oz beef
   steak, cut into cubes
½ small red pepper, chopped

pinch paprika pepper
3–4 tablespoons soured cream
   or Greek yogurt
salt and freshly ground black
   pepper

Heat a little butter in a heavy nonstick pan, add the onion and cook, stirring frequently, until softened. Add the steak cubes and red pepper and cook, stirring occasionally, for about 4 minutes. Sprinkle the paprika over and stir to coat all the ingredients then stir in the soured cream or yogurt and heat gently for about 2 minutes. Season to taste.

Quick-fried Kidneys with Vegetables

A well-flavoured dish that takes only minutes to cook using the oriental stir-fry method but not the flavourings.

2 lamb's kidneys
small piece onion or shallot
3 tablespoons medium-bodied red wine
few drops lemon juice
1 small clove garlic, finely chopped
olive oil

freshly ground black pepper
1 small carrot, cut into strips
approximately 40g/1½oz mangetout
finely chopped fresh parsley (optional)
salt

Cut out the cores and tough tubing from the kidneys with kitchen scissors, leaving each kidney whole.

Using a garlic press squeeze out 1 teaspoon juice from the onion or shallot into a small bowl. Stir in the wine, lemon juice, garlic, 1 teaspoon olive oil, and black pepper. Add the kidneys, turn over in the liquid and leave to marinate for about 30 minutes.

Remove the kidneys from the marinade, allowing the excess to drain off; pat dry. Heat a little oil over a high heat in a heavy-based frying pan, add the carrot, and gently stir the strips around the pan until they go limp.

Scoop out on to absorbent paper. Add the mangetout to the pan then add the kidneys and quickly sear on all sides. Remove the kidneys and reduce the heat a little under the pan. Using a sharp knife, slice the kidneys into pieces – they will still be raw inside.

Pour the marinade into the pan and boil until almost completely evaporated. Return the kidneys and vegetables to the pan and stir-fry for about 30 seconds until evenly glossed. Sprinkle with a little parsley, if using, and salt and serve immediately.

VARIATIONS

- Substitute other vegetables, such as courgette and red pepper, for the carrot and mangetout.
- Substitute approximately 115g/4oz sliced lamb's liver for the kidneys.

_____ *Warm Kidney and Cabbage Salad* _____
with Mustard Dressing

30g/1oz unsalted butter
1 tablespoon olive oil
2 lamb's kidneys, cored
¼ Savoy cabbage, thinly sliced
1 small clove garlic, finely
  chopped

2 teaspoons Dijon mustard
2 teaspoons sherry vinegar
salt and freshly ground black
  pepper

Heat a small nut of the butter with 1 teaspoon of the oil in a small, heavy frying pan, add the kidneys and cook for about 2 minutes per side, so they remain pink in the centre. Using a slotted spoon, transfer to a warmed plate and keep warm.

Add the remaining butter to the pan then stir in the cabbage and garlic and cook over a moderate heat, stirring occasionally, for 4–5 minutes.

Meanwhile, blend the mustard and vinegar together then gradually beat in the remaining oil. Season to taste.

Season the cabbage and place in a mound on a warmed plate. Thickly slice the kidneys, season them and place on the cabbage. Stir any juices that seeped from the kidneys on to the plate into the dressing then pour over the kidneys and cabbage.

Kidney, Liver and Bacon

Serve on bread that has either been toasted slowly or baked in the oven until it is crisp (brioche is particularly good), so that it absorbs the flavourful, savoury juices.

1 teaspoon oil
nut unsalted butter
1 slice smoked back bacon, cut into strips about 0.5cm/¼in wide
85g/3oz lamb's kidneys, cut into strips about 0.5cm/¼in wide
85g/3oz lamb's liver, cut into strips about 0.5cm/¼in wide
1 clove garlic, thinly sliced
salt and freshly ground black pepper
approximately ½ teaspoon wholegrain mustard
approximately 1½ tablespoons double cream
1 teaspoon finely chopped fresh tarragon, or 2 teaspoons chopped fresh parsley or coriander

Heat the oil and a very small nut of butter in a frying pan, add the bacon and cook until it just begins to go crisp. Add the kidney and liver and cook quickly until beginning to brown. Reduce the heat to very low, add a little more butter, the garlic and seasoning. Cover and cook gently for 20–25 minutes. Add the mustard and cream to the pan and bubble for 2 minutes or until thickened. Add the tarragon, parsley or coriander and adjust the seasoning and mustard to taste.

VARIATION
• Use Greek yogurt or fromage blanc instead of cream, but do not allow the sauce to boil afterwards.

Mustard-stuffed Kidneys
in a Ham Jacket

2 lamb's kidneys
1 tablespoon fresh
  breadcrumbs
mustard
lemon juice
salt and freshly ground black
  pepper

1 slice Parma ham or
  prosciutto
a little oil and butter
1–2 tablespoons medium-
  bodied dry white wine
  (optional)

Skin the kidneys then, using sharp scissors, cut out the core from each one to make a pocket. Mix the breadcrumbs with approximately ¼ teaspoon mustard then moisten with ½–1 teaspoon lemon juice. Add black pepper and just a little salt. Divide between the pockets in the kidneys. Spread a little mustard over the ham, cut into two and wrap a piece round each kidney, enclosing them completely.

Heat a little oil and butter in a small nonstick pan. Add the kidney parcels and cook over a high heat for 4 minutes, turning halfway through.

Using a slotted spoon, transfer the kidneys to a warmed plate. Stir the wine, if using, into the cooking juices, bring to the boil, and allow to bubble until slightly reduced. Season with black pepper then pour over the kidneys. If not using wine, simply season the cooking juices and pour them over the kidneys.

Sausages with Red Cabbage

Always robust and satisfying, the character of this dish can be changed quite substantially according to what type of sausage is used. It could be herby, full of garlic or hot spices, mild, such as Italian luganega, or have the slight gaminess of venison. This is a simple dish and, like many simple dishes, its success depends on using good-quality ingredients – in this case good, coarse-grained, meaty sausages.

2 tablespoons olive oil
1 small clove garlic, crushed
115–150g/4–5oz red cabbage, thinly sliced
pinch caraway seeds (optional)

approximately 115g/4oz sausage, cut into 7.5cm/3in lengths if appropriate
salt and freshly ground black pepper

Heat the oil in a saucepan, add the garlic and cook, stirring occasionally, until turning golden. Stir in the cabbage and caraway seeds, if using, making sure the cabbage is well coated with oil then cook, stirring occasionally, until slightly softened.

Meanwhile pierce each piece of sausage two or thee times with the point of a sharp knife then fry in a small nonstick pan until evenly browned.

Arrange the pieces of sausage in the cabbage, sprinkle with a little salt and pepper, cover and continue to cook for about 20 minutes.

VARIATIONS
- If using venison sausages, add some redcurrant jelly to the pan with the cabbage.
- Substitute hard white cabbage for red cabbage and serve with a warmed mustard vinaigrette.

Desserts

Behind the doors of my store cupboard I keep a selection of pots, jars and packets to spark off ideas for new dishes and to provide variety and flavour for desserts and sweet snacks as well as savoury ones. Favourite items include jars of brandy or rum butter for making luxurious toast, topping baked apples, pears or bananas (which could also be grilled or sautéed) or poached rhubarb, plums or gooseberries; individual flower honeys and honeys flavoured with ginger or vanilla pods for sweetening cooked fruits, topping grilled grapefruit or milk puddings, or spreading on toast etc.; rose-water and orange flower water, dried fruits (apples, pears, apricots, peaches, figs and prunes) and preserved stem ginger.

Fruits canned in natural juice can be very useful for making crumbles, sundae-type dishes, sorbets, ice-creams, sauces, toppings for biscuits, buns or bread, or for filling pancakes and sweet omelettes.

Fruit

Fruit provides a very simple dessert, which nevertheless can be made that bit more special with very little effort – for example by combining two different fruits (useful if you have something like half a pear to use up), or adding complementary flavourings:

Bananas   Go well with almonds, orange juice, rum and spices; top with Greek yogurt.

Blackcurrants   Go well with pears or mint.

Lychees   Delicious with raspberries or chocolate.

Melon   Toss with some chopped preserved stem ginger, or with some raspberries, and sprinkle a few drops of orange flower water over.

Oranges   Sprinkle with a few drops of orange flower water.

Peaches   Good with rose-water, anything almond-flavoured, such as Amaretti, and raspberries and redcurrants.

Pears   Combine with blackcurrants or raspberries; sprinkle with chopped preserved stem ginger.

Pineapple   Serve with mint – chopped fresh leaves with caster sugar – or with crème de menthe, gin, orange juice and muscovado sugar, or with fresh lime juice and dark rum.

Raspberries   Go with melon and pears, and also with rose-water or dark chocolate (try topping raspberries with cream or fresh cream cheese flavoured with rose-water, and serving with dark chocolate cake, bitter chocolate mints, or grated dark chocolate).

Strawberries   Sprinkle with orange flower water or orange juice.

—————— *Stuffed Nectarine* ——————

approximately 2 heaped teaspoons chopped dried apricots

2 tablespoons medium-bodied dry white wine

2 tablespoons soft cheese

1 nectarine

2 mint leaves, for garnish

Gently simmer the apricots in the wine in a small covered saucepan until tender. Remove from the heat and leave to cool. Purée then add the soft cheese and mix until just blended. Cover and chill.

Cut the nectarine in half and remove the stone. Fill the cavities with the apricot mixture. Garnish with the mint leaves.

VARIATIONS
- Add 1–2 teaspoons orange liqueur to the filling.
- Use a peach instead of a nectarine.

Spicy Rum Banana

This dessert seems like a real treat but it is not expensive, nor is it difficult when made for one person, although it can be more exacting for larger numbers.

1½ tablespoons orange juice
1 teaspoon orange rind
very small pinch each ground
    cinnamon and ground
    nutmeg

1 banana
unsalted butter
1½ teaspoons soft light brown
    sugar
1 tablespoon dark rum

Mix the orange juice, rind and spices together.

Peel the banana then slice it lengthways 2 or 3 times to within 2.5cm/1in of one end, to enable you to fan it out.

Melt a little butter in a small frying pan, add the banana and cook gently on both sides until a light golden brown.

Sprinkle the sugar over, pour in the spiced orange juice and heat through for 2–3 minutes. Transfer the banana to a warmed plate and pour over the sauce.

Warm the rum in a metal spoon over a flame, or heat it in a small pan, ignite it then while it is still flaming, carefully pour it over the banana. Eat immediately.

VARIATIONS
- Sprinkle a few toasted flaked almonds over.
- Change the spices – try Chinese five-spice powder for an interesting difference.

Sliced Orange Salad

This is a delicious fresh, light dessert when eaten plain, but you could also serve it with some chilled Greek yogurt, fromage blanc or quark.

1 orange   few drops orange flower water
few crushed cardamom seeds   (optional)

Using a small, sharp knife and working over a small bowl to catch the juice, remove all the peel and white pith from the orange. Cut the orange into thin slices and arrange on a plate. Pour over the juice from the bowl and sprinkle with the crushed cardamom seeds and the orange flower water, if using. Cover and chill lightly.

VARIATIONS
- Use ground cinnamon, ground cloves or crushed, toasted coriander seeds instead of cardamom.
- Instead of sprinkling spice over the orange, add a very small pinch of ground cinnamon mixed with a little sugar to some Greek yogurt, fromage blanc or quark. Spoon on to the orange slices and scatter chopped hazelnuts and finely shredded orange rind over.
- For chilly nights – put the orange slices on a heatproof plate or in a heatproof dish, sprinkle a little brown sugar over and brown lightly under a hot grill instead of chilling.

Simple Grilled Pear

A quick, warming, but light, pud. Serve with yogurt, fromage blanc, ice-cream, crème fraîche, or cream, if liked.

1 ripe pear   melted unsalted butter
lemon juice   caster sugar

Peel the pear, cut in half lengthways and remove the core. Brush
all over with lemon juice. Place the halves cut-side down on a
heatproof dish and slice thinly almost to the necks. Push down
lightly on each half so that it fans out then brush with a little
melted butter and sprinkle with a little sugar. Grill under a hot
grill until the pear is light golden and warmed through.

VARIATIONS

- Sprinkle over a little ground spice, such as ginger, cinnamon
  or mixed spice.
- Spoon over a little cognac or poire William.

Caramelized Apple

1 Cox's Orange Pippin   pinch ground cinnamon
unsalted butter, preferably   Greek yogurt, fromage blanc,
  clarified   vanilla ice-cream, or cream,
1 tablespoon sugar   to serve

Peel the apple, remove the core, then cut the fruit into thick
slices. Melt a small knob of butter in a heavy pan, add the apple
slices in a single layer and cook slowly until a light golden brown
underneath. Turn the slices over carefully and brown the other
side. Mix the sugar and cinnamon together, sprinkle over the
apple and cook gently until the sugar just begins to turn to
caramel.

Transfer to a warmed plate and serve with Greek yogurt,
fromage blanc, ice-cream or cream.

VARIATION

- Serve the apple slices on bread, sweet bread or brioche, toasted
  and buttered, or buttered then baked in the oven until crisp.

Fresh Apricots in Wine

Apricots that are disappointingly lacking in juiciness and sun-ripened flavour can be gently poached in lightly sweetened white wine, which makes them tender and brings out their taste.

approximately 175g/6oz fresh
  apricots
55–85ml/2–3fl oz medium-
  bodied dry white wine

seeds from 1 cardamom pod,
  crushed
sugar
lemon juice (optional)

In a small, covered saucepan, gently poach the apricots in the wine with the cardamom seeds and a little sugar for 5–8 minutes or until just tender. Leave to cool in the cooking liquor. Add a little lemon juice to lift the flavour, if necessary.

Blackberries and Apples in Port

The quantity below is enough for two servings, which can be eaten hot or cold.

approximately 225g/8oz
  cooking apples, preferably
  Bramley's
1 tablespoon port

approximately 85g/3oz
  blackberries
sugar (optional)
cream, Greek yogurt, fromage
  blanc or ice-cream, to serve

Peel, core and slice the apples then cook with the port in a covered pan over a low heat until tender but still retaining their shape. Add the blackberries and cook for about 2 minutes until they just stain the apples. Add sugar to taste, if necessary.

Serve hot or cold with cream, Greek yogurt, fromage blanc or ice-cream.

VARIATIONS

- Leave the second portion to cool then blend with yogurt or cream to make a fool. Serve chilled.
- Use the second portion to make a fruit Crumble or Crisp (see pages 233–4).
- Serve with pain perdu (see page 230).

——————— *Dried Fruit Compote* ———————

This is just as good eaten for breakfast or to end a meal. For a clean, fresh contrast to the richness of the dried fruits, serve with citrus segments, chopped apples or pears, or halved grapes. Crème fraîche, soured cream, Greek yogurt or fromage blanc are good accompaniments.

Makes approximately 2–3 servings.

175g/6oz mixed dried fruit, either bought ready mixed, or your own combination of, for example, pears, peaches, apricots, apple rings and prunes

300ml/½ pint cold tea
1 lemon
finely grated rind and juice 1 orange
approximately 1 teaspoon orange flower water

Soak all the fruit except the apple rings in the tea overnight, or for a day.

Pare the rind from the lemon in a long strip, and squeeze the juice from the lemon. Mix with the soaked dried fruit, the apple rings, if using, and the orange rind and juice. Cook covered in a small pan over a very low heat, stirring two or three times, until the fruit is as tender as you like it. Remove the lemon rind and stir in orange flower water to taste. Serve warm or cold.

VARIATIONS

- Soak the fruit in orange or apple juice instead of tea; pare the rind from the orange in a long strip and add to the fruit.

- Add a 2.5cm/1in piece cinnamon stick and 2 cloves to the fruit before cooking, and omit the orange flower water.
- Add some grated fresh root ginger or chopped preserved stem ginger to the fruit either before cooking or afterwards.
- A no-cook method of preparation is to put the fruits into a bowl, pour orange or apple juice over, add the orange flower water and a few drops of almond essence, cover and leave in the refrigerator for 48 hours, turning the fruit occasionally. Add flavourings as above, if liked.

Strawberry Omelette

This is for giving yourself a treat in the summer, when strawberries are at their best.

175g/6oz strawberries
few drops orange flower water
caster sugar
1 egg, separated

1 tablespoon Greek yogurt, fromage blanc or whipped cream
small knob butter
icing sugar

Purée half the strawberries with orange flower water and sugar to taste. Chop the remaining strawberries then gently heat in a small, covered saucepan, shaking the pan occasionally, until softened.

Beat the egg yolk with the yogurt, fromage blanc or whipped cream and a small pinch of sugar. Whisk the egg white until stiff but not dry then carefully fold into the egg yolk mixture until just evenly blended.

Heat the butter in a small omelette pan or frying pan, add the egg mixture and cook over a moderate heat until the underneath is lightly coloured and the top is beginning to set but is still moist and fluffy – this happens quite quickly so take care not to let the omelette overcook. Place the warmed strawberries on the omelette and fold in half.

Either pour the strawberry purée on to a warmed plate and slide the omelette on top, or pour the purée over the omelette. Sprinkle with icing sugar.

VARIATIONS

- Add a little orange liqueur to the strawberries instead of orange flower water.
- Glaze the top of the omelette by sprinkling a little sieved icing sugar over the surface of the folded omelette while still in the pan and placing under a hot grill.

——————— *Poached Dried Apricots* ———————

Nowadays, more and more of the dried apricots available have been treated so that they do not need to be soaked, but for this type of dish I prefer to use ones that need to be plumped and softened overnight, as they have a better flavour and texture. Serve the poached apricots as they are, or use as a filling for pancakes, to top slices of sweet bread or cake, or over ice-cream.

20g/¾oz peeled fresh root ginger, cut along the grain into fine shreds
115g/4oz dried apricots, soaked overnight

rind ½ small lemon, cut into fine strips
cream, crème fraîche, ordinary or Greek yogurt, or fromage blanc, to serve

In a small pan simmer the ginger in 300 ml/½ pint water for 5 minutes. Drain the apricots then add to the pan with the lemon rind. Lower the heat and cook gently, uncovered, for about 25 minutes or until the apricots are tender.

Using a slotted spoon, transfer the apricots to a bowl then boil the liquid until it becomes syrupy. Pour over the apricots.

Serve warm, or leave to cool then chill lightly. Serve with cream, crème fraîche, yogurt or fromage blanc.

VARIATIONS
- Boil the syrup for slightly longer so that it becomes thicker, remove from the heat then add a little brandy, whisky, or rum.
- Use orange rind instead of lemon rind.
- Apricots with Vanilla – substitute 150ml/¼ pint apple juice for half the water, omit the ginger and lemon rind and add half a vanilla pod. After poaching the apricots, cut 1.25cm/½in from the vanilla pod, open it out and scrape the seeds into the poaching liquid. Boil until thickened. Wash and dry the remaining vanilla pod for re-use.

Pears Poached in Vanilla Syrup _____ _with Fresh Raspberry Sauce_

1 ripe pear
30g/1oz sugar
approximately 1.25cm/½in length vanilla pod, slit lengthways
small strip lemon rind

approximately 55g/2oz raspberries
lemon juice (optional)
fromage blanc, crème fraîche, Greek yogurt or ice-cream, to serve

Peel the pear, cut in half and remove the core and fibrous strip. Gently heat the sugar in 115ml/4fl oz water in a small saucepan in which the pear halves will just fit lying down. Add the vanilla pod and lemon rind then increase the heat and bring to the boil. Add the pear halves, lower the heat and cook gently, uncovered, until just tender – about 5 minutes.

Using a slotted spoon, transfer the pear to a dish. Purée the raspberries with about 2 teaspoons of the syrup, adding a little lemon juice to lift the flavour, if necessary. Pass through a sieve then pour over the pear. Cover and chill. Serve with fromage blanc, crème fraîche, Greek yogurt or ice-cream.

VARIATION
- Simple Pear Compote – cut the peeled and cored pear into slices and poach in a small pan in a single layer, just covered by water, until just tender, turning them over to ensure they cook evenly. Using a slotted spoon, transfer the pear slices to a dish and sprinkle a little orange juice over. Leave to cool.

Cream Crowdie

1 tablespoon oatmeal
70ml/2½fl oz double cream
approximately 1 tablespoon whisky

1 tablespoon clear honey
85g/3oz raspberries

Toast the oatmeal under a grill until an even golden brown, stirring it around occasionally to make sure it colours evenly.

Whip the cream until soft peaks are formed. Mix the whisky with the honey then stir into the cream with the oatmeal.

Reserve a few raspberries. Layer the remaining raspberries with the cream mixture in a glass dish. Cover and chill then return to room temperature about 30 minutes before eating. Decorate with the reserved raspberries.

VARIATION
- If raspberries are not available, simply spoon the oatmeal mixture into a glass and scatter a little chopped preserved stem ginger over.

Rose Cream

This is a rich dessert that is completed to perfection by fresh raspberries or raspberry purée. It can be cooked on the bottom shelf of the oven at the same time as Potato and Celeriac Dauphinoise (see page 127).

approximately 2 teaspoons
  sugar
115ml/4fl oz single cream or
  half milk and half double
  cream

1 egg yolk or 1 small egg,
  lightly beaten
few drops rose-water

In a small pan gently warm the sugar in the cream, or cream and milk, slowly stirring with a wooden spoon until dissolved then bring to the boil. Remove the skin from the surface then slowly pour on to the egg yolk or egg in a bowl, stirring slowly. Add a few drops of rose-water to taste.

Stand a buttered heatproof dish (approximately 11cm/4in wide) in a baking tin then pour the cream mixture into the dish and pour boiling water in the tin. Bake at 150°C/300°F/gas mark 2 for about 30–35 minutes until lightly set in the centre.

Carefully remove the dish from the baking tin, leave to cool then chill in the fridge.

Light Lime Soufflé

This light pudding is very easy and quick to prepare and makes a refreshing end to a meal.

85g/3oz Ricotta cheese, sieved
finely grated rind 1 lime
approximately 1 tablespoon
  lime juice

approximately 2 teaspoons
  caster sugar
1 small egg white

Beat the cheese with the lime rind, juice, and sugar to taste. Whisk the egg white until stiff but not dry then gently fold into the lime mixture until just evenly blended. Transfer to a small buttered heatproof dish and bake at 190°/375°F/gas mark 5 for about 12 minutes, or steam for 8–10 minutes in a steaming basket, colander or sieve placed over a pan of boiling water. Eat immediately.

Instant Mock Cheesecake

Spread biscuits such as shortbread, digestive or chocolate with fromage blanc or Greek yogurt then top with any fresh or dried fruit you have available – strawberries, raspberries, blackcurrants, lychees, apricots, plums, cherries, mandarin segments, poached dried apricots, or fruits preserved in alcohol. Sprinkle the fruit with rose-water or orange flower water, eau de vie, whisky, brandy or any appropriate liqueur.

Soft Cheese and Fruit Sundae

approximately 55g/2oz soft
  cheese
milk (optional)

caster sugar or honey
fruit

Beat the soft cheese with a little milk, if liked, to loosen the texture, add a little sugar or honey to taste then layer in a glass with the fruit of your choice, finishing with a dollop of soft cheese.

VARIATION
- Include layers of crushed biscuits, macaroons, Amaretti biscuits, or lightly fried breadcrumbs with a touch of spice added, if you like.

Raspberry Ripple

Have the raspberries, yogurt and fromage blanc or quark chilled. Serve with Pompadour fan wafers or crisp biscuits.

85g/3oz raspberries
55ml/2fl oz Greek yogurt
2 tablespoons fromage blanc
  or quark

caster sugar
rose-water (optional)
small mint leaves, for garnish

Purée 55g/2oz of the raspberries and pass through a sieve. Mix the yogurt with the fromage blanc or quark and add sugar and rose-water, if using, to taste.

Spoon the raspberry purée through the quark to give a ripple effect. Put all the remaining raspberries except one into a glass, spoon on the rippled mixture and place the reserved raspberry on top. Decorate with small mint leaves.

VARIATIONS
- Sprinkle a little eau de vie de framboise over the 30g/1oz of raspberries in the glass. Leave to soak for a while, if possible, before adding the topping.
- Add a crumbled macaroon to the raspberries in the glass.

Mocha Honeycomb

This is a light, lightly set pudding that is well worth the little bit of effort required to prepare it – it is so much more wholesome than similar commercial products in plastic pots.

1 egg, separated	1½ teaspoons instant coffee
approximately 2 teaspoons sugar	115ml/4fl oz milk
	1 teaspoon gelatine
2 drops vanilla essence	scant 30g/1oz grated chocolate

Mix the egg yolk, sugar, vanilla essence and instant coffee together. Bring the milk to the boil in a small nonstick saucepan then stir into the egg yolk mixture. Pour back into the pan and heat very gently, stirring with a wooden spoon, until thick enough to coat the back of the spoon. Do not allow to boil otherwise it will curdle. Leave to cool.

Sprinkle the gelatine over 1 tablespoon water in a small bowl. Leave for about 5 minutes then place the bowl over a saucepan of hot water and heat gently, stirring occasionally, until the gelatine dissolves. Remove from the heat, cool slightly then stir into the coffee-flavoured custard.

Whisk the egg white until stiff but not dry then lightly fold into the custard. Leave until just beginning to set. Lightly fold the grated chocolate through, spoon into a serving dish and leave to set completely.

VARIATIONS
- Coffee Honeycomb – omit the chocolate and sprinkle some fine threads of orange rind over the honeycomb to decorate.
- Coconut and Coffee Honeycomb – omit the chocolate and add desiccated coconut with the milk.
- Lemon, Lime or Orange Honeycomb – omit the coffee and chocolate, add 2 tablespoons lemon, lime or orange juice to the honeycomb after it has cooled.

———————— *Chocolate Mousse* ————————

This is the first chocolate mousse recipe that I made; it is very simple and straightforward and I have never found a better one.

55g/2oz good-quality plain or bitter chocolate, chopped
very small knob unsalted butter (optional)

1 egg, separated
cognac or eau de vie de framboise (optional)

Melt the chocolate, with the butter if using (it makes the mousse more shiny), in a bowl placed over a saucepan of hot, not boiling water. Remove from the heat, stir the egg yolk into the chocolate, and flavour with a few drops of cognac or eau de vie de framboise, if liked. Whisk the egg white until stiff but not dry and gently fold into the chocolate mixture until just evenly blended. Transfer to a serving dish and leave to set for at least 30 minutes, preferably in the refrigerator. Cover and keep in the refrigerator if eating later.

———————— *Nutty Omelette* ————————

unsalted butter
approximately 1 tablespoon flaked almonds
approximately 1 tablespoon crushed walnuts

pinch sugar mixed with a touch of spice
2 eggs

In a small pan, heat a small nut of butter, add the almonds and cook until beginning to turn golden. Add the walnuts and spiced sugar and cook, stirring frequently, until the sugar has melted and the nuts are well coated.

Make the omelette in a separate pan (see page 69). Spoon the nuts and their butter on to the omelette, fold it over quickly and eat immediately.

Bread-based Desserts

Toasted fruit buns, teacakes, crumpets, muffins, and slices of cake, fruit loaf or brioche can be used as the basis of sweet snacks and desserts; or looked at another way, these recipes are useful for using up any buns, cake etc.

———————— *Apricot Toast* ————————

1 slice fruit cake, sweet fruit
   loaf or malt loaf
soft cheese or cottage cheese

1 large, ripe apricot, or 2
   apricot halves canned in
   natural juice
soft brown sugar

Lightly toast both sides of the cake or loaf. Spread one side with soft cheese or cottage cheese. Stone and slice the apricot, or simply slice if canned, and arrange the slices over the cheese. Sprinkle soft brown sugar over the top and place under a hot grill until the sugar has melted and glazed the fruit.

———————— *Cinnamon Pear Bun* ————————

This recipe makes quite a substantial sweet snack, so halve the quantities if you prefer, and use the remaining pear half for another recipe, such as Pear Vinaigrette (see page 236) or instead of apple in Red Cabbage and Apple Salad (see page 63).

Canned pear in natural juice could be used instead of fresh pear.

1 fruit bun, cut in half
unsalted butter
small pinch ground cinnamon

1 pear, peeled and cored
soft brown sugar

Toast the bun on both sides then spread the cut sides generously with butter and sprinkle ground cinnamon over. Slice the pear thickly then arrange the slices on the bun. Sprinkle with soft brown sugar and grill until the sugar has melted.

Mincemeat Muffin

1 muffin
1–2 tablespoons mincemeat

lemon juice
softened unsalted butter

Split the muffin. Mix the mincemeat with a good squeeze of lemon juice then spoon into the muffin. Brush or spread the butter over the outside of the muffin then toast.

Spiced Sesame Toast

Make extra spiced butter and keep covered in the fridge for spreading on toast, buns etc.

small pinch mixed spice,
   cinnamon or cardamom
small pinch brown sugar

unsalted butter
1 slice bread
sesame seeds

Blend the spice and sugar with sufficient butter to spread over the toast. Toast one side of the bread, spread with the spiced butter and sprinkle sesame seeds generously over. Toast until browned.

————— *Fig and Honey Croissant* —————

If fresh figs are not available, use drained canned figs if they have been canned in natural juice.

1 large croissant
15g/½oz unsalted butter
7 chopped walnut halves
3 teaspoons clear honey

1 tablespoon dark rum
1 teaspoon lemon juice
2–3 ripe figs, depending on
   size, quartered

Slice the croissant in half lengthways and toast on both sides.

Meanwhile, melt the butter in a small pan, add the chopped walnuts and cook, stirring occasionally, until golden. Remove and reserve a few of the nuts. Over a low heat stir 2 tablespoons of the honey, the rum and the lemon juice into the nuts in the pan. When evenly mixed, gently stir in the figs.

Spoon the fig mixture on to the bottom half of the croissant, cover with the other half, brush with the remaining honey and sprinkle the reserved nuts over.

Banana- and Nut-filled Croissant

Moist, light but quite substantial.

1 small banana
approximately 1½ teaspoons
   lemon juice
1 teaspoon grated lemon rind
1½ teaspoons ground almonds

small pinch each mixed spice
   and ground ginger
1 walnut half, chopped
1 large croissant
beaten egg
flaked almonds

Peel the banana then mash with the lemon juice and rind. Stir the ground almonds and spices together then stir into the mashed banana with the chopped walnut.

Cut a slit along the outer curved side of the croissant then carefully cut a pocket. Fill the pocket with the banana mixture, place on a greased baking sheet, brush with beaten egg and sprinkle the flaked almonds over. Place beneath a moderate grill until the banana mixture and croissant are warmed through and the almonds on top are toasted. Adjust the position of the croissant or reduce the heat if the top browns too quickly.

VARIATIONS
- Use orange or lime juice and rind instead of lemon juice.
- Try different spices.
- The walnut can be replaced by an almond, cashew nut or pecan half.

Fig Gratin

1 fairly thin slice of cake such
  as Madeira or panettone
brandy
1 ripe fig
3–4 tablespoons soured

cream, crème fraîche or
  Greek yogurt, chilled
demerara sugar
flaked almonds

Lay the cake in a small heatproof dish and sprinkle a little brandy over. Thinly slice the fig and arrange on the cake. Spoon the soured cream, crème fraîche or yogurt over, sprinkle with a little demerara sugar and a few flaked almonds then place under a hot grill until golden.

Pain Perdu

This simple dessert answers to many names, including French Toast and Poor Knights of Windsor. There are even more variations to the recipe than there are names. The egg can be flavoured with vanilla essence and the spice omitted; cream, fromage blanc or Ricotta cheese can be mixed with the egg yolk instead of milk, or the alcohol can be omitted.

The quality of bread determines how good the dish will taste – brioche and other enriched breads are very good and fruit loaf makes an interesting variation.

1 whole small egg, or 1 small
  egg yolk
milk
1 slice bread, crusts removed

sweet sherry or Madeira
  (optional)
unsalted butter
sugar mixed with grated
  nutmeg, or other spice

Beat the egg or egg yolk with a little milk, using more milk if just the yolk is used. Soak the bread in this mixture then remove, allowing the excess to drain off, and sprinkle with a little sherry or Madeira, if using. Fry in hot butter until crisp and light golden.

Drain on absorbent paper and sprinkle with sugar mixed with a little grated nutmeg.

VARIATIONS

- Omit the sugar and spice and serve with a sauce of plain chocolate melted with a little water.
- Omit the sugar and spice and serve with jam spooned on.
- Omit the spice and serve topped with fruit, either raw, such as strawberries, or cooked, such as poached apple or pear or dried fruits.

———— Bread and Butter Pudding ————

If you steam the pudding, cover the dish loosely with greaseproof paper to prevent the condensation that gathers on the lid of the steamer dripping on the pudding.

unsalted butter
1–2 slices of bread, crusts removed
1½ tablespoons dried fruit e.g. apricots, raisins, sultanas, roughly chopped if necessary

1 small egg
115ml/4 fl oz milk
2–3 teaspoons caster or soft brown sugar
small pinch freshly grated nutmeg

Butter the bread then cut out a circle from one slice to fit inside a ramekin or other heatproof dish and reserve for the top of the pudding. Butter the dish and line the base with some of the bread, buttered-side uppermost. Scatter some of the fruit over, cover with more bread, scatter some of the fruit over this then top with the circle of bread. Lightly beat the egg, milk, sugar and grated nutmeg together then strain over the bread and leave to stand for 20–30 minutes.

Either steam the pudding for 30 minutes or place in a baking tin, pour boiling water in the tin and bake at 180°C/350°F/gas mark 4 for 30 minutes.

VARIATIONS

- Include a little chopped mixed peel with the dried fruit.
- Use another spice instead of nutmeg e.g. cinnamon, cardamom, mixed spice.
- Use some chopped preserved stem ginger, finely grated root ginger or orange or lemon rind instead of nutmeg.
- Substitute a drop or two of vanilla essence for the spice.
- Flavour with a little whisky, brandy, rum, sherry or liqueur added to the egg and milk.
- After buttering the bread, spread with marmalade – my choice is a bitter, chunky one.
- Treat yourself to a more luxurious pudding and use single, whipping or double cream instead of milk.

Autumn Pudding

40g/1½oz mixed dried fruit, such as apricots, pears, peaches, apples
approximately 115ml/4fl oz tea, apple juice or orange juice

approximately 2 slices bread, crusts removed
cream, Greek yogurt, fromage blanc or ice-cream, to serve

In a small pan gently poach the dried fruit in the tea or fruit juice until soft, adding more liquid if necessary so that 2–3 tablespoons remain when the fruit is cooked. Meanwhile roll out the bread with a rolling pin then line a ramekin dish with most of it, cutting it as necessary and leaving some to make a lid. Fill the dish with the fruit, cover with the remaining bread and spoon the fruit juices over. Place a small saucer or piece of clingfilm on top then place a weight on this. Leave overnight in the fridge or a cool place.

Unmould and serve with cream, Greek yogurt, fromage blanc, or ice-cream.

Crumbles

Sweet crumbles, like their savoury counterparts, are easy to make. The amount given below is enough for one serving, but extra can be made and kept in a covered container in the refrigerator for making quick puddings. Crumbles are good cold as well as hot, so I usually cook sufficient for two servings, one to eat hot, the other cold. If you want to warm up a portion of crumble, either leave it in the dish in which it was baked or transfer it to a heatproof bowl, cover and place over a saucepan of simmering water until hot.

The traditional accompaniment for crumble is, of course, custard but more convenient alternatives that are just as good to eat are cream, ice-cream and yogurt, especially Greek yogurt.

20g/¾oz hard margarine or butter
40g/1½oz flour
pinch salt

approximately 1½ tablespoons sugar – white or brown
115g/4oz prepared fruit – fresh or canned and drained

Cut the margarine or butter into small pieces then rub into the flour, salt and sugar in a bowl until the mixture resembles fine breadcrumbs. Put the prepared fruit into a buttered small oven-proof dish, cover with the crumble mixture, press it down lightly and score the top with the prongs of a fork. Bake at 180°C/350°F/gas mark 4 for about 25 minutes or until the top is crisp and golden, and the fruit cooked.

VARIATIONS

- · Substitute rolled oats for half of the flour for a more crunchy texture.
- Include some chopped nuts or sesame seeds in the topping for added crunch.
- Stir 2 teaspoons desiccated coconut into the topping for a chewy texture.
- Reduce the sugar and flour slightly and add some crushed digestive biscuits.
- Flavour the crumble topping with a pinch of finely grated lemon or orange rind, or a small pinch of crushed cardamom seeds, ground mixed spice or grated root ginger.
- Sprinkle over the top chopped nuts, sesame seeds, rolled oats or sweetened breadcrumbs dotted with butter.
- Muesli Crumble – use 40g/1½oz flour mixed with 30g/1oz unsweetened muesli, and reduce the sugar to ¾–1 tablespoon.

Crisp

A crisp is even easier and quicker to make than a crumble. It involves no more than mixing breadcrumbs with sugar to taste (about 40–55g/1½–2oz breadcrumbs with 1–2 tablespoons of sugar) then preferably adding a little mixed spice, nutmeg or crushed cardamom seeds. Spread this mixture over the filling, dot with butter, or dribble melted butter over, and cook at 180°C/350°F/gas mark 4 for about 25 minutes or until the top is brown and crisp and the filling cooked.

VARIATIONS
- See Crumbles.
- Almond Crisp – replace half the breadcrumbs with an equal amount of ground almonds, mix together with the sugar then rub in 15–20g/½–¾oz butter.

SAUCES, BUTTERS AND STOCKS

Vinaigrette

I use the term vinaigrette in a loose sense – rather than the classic French dressing of vinegar, olive oil and herbs, I mean an acid-based dressing that can be varied enormously to tone with the salad ingredients and create different effects. The character of a salad can be changed simply by changing the dressing – this is no more complicated than adding a little grated orange rind or grated root ginger, perhaps a pinch of toasted cardamom seeds, a few drops of soy sauce, some horseradish for a palate-livening 'kick', or cream, fromage blanc or yogurt to temper it.

The vinegar can be white wine, fine, mild Champagne, more robust red or deep, full-flavoured sherry or balsamic. Fruit juice, usually citrus, can be used instead of vinegar, or a combination of both. Similarly, there are many oils that can be used for variety – different-flavoured olive oils, from mild pure oil through to fruity, green extra-virgin; walnut and hazelnut oils, or sesame with its toasty, rich, warm flavour. It is best to use the last three with a less distinctive oil otherwise their flavour will dominate the salad.

The basic proportions for a vinaigrette are commonly quoted as three parts oil to one part vinegar, but this should only be taken as a rough guide; the proportions can be adjusted to take into account the type of salad and its individual components, and the other ingredients in the dressing. Vinegars vary in their acidity, oils in their strength. Most vinaigrettes are easy to make in small quantities, either by whisking the ingredients together in a small bowl, or shaking them in a tightly closed screw-top jar, but they also keep well in the refrigerator. Beat or shake the dressing before using.

Pear Vinaigrette

An unusual way of using up half a pear (see pages 195, 226 for other ideas). It goes with crisp salads of smoked pork, chicken or eel, prosciutto crudo, such as Parma ham, or simply tossed with endive or chicory and pine nuts or walnuts.

½ ripe pear, peeled and cored
approximately ½ teaspoon
    finely grated lime or lemon
    rind
1 teaspoon olive oil

1 scant tablespoon medium-
    bodied dry white wine
    (optional)
salt and freshly ground white
    pepper

Purée all the ingredients together, substituting 1 scant tablespoon water for the wine if necessary. Chill.

VARIATION
• Use half nut oil (walnut or hazelnut) and half olive oil.

Red Pepper Vinaigrette

Serve over cold broccoli, fennel or French beans – add some sliced anchovy fillets and black olives for a delicious salad – or with poached white fish or trout, or plainly cooked chicken.

1 red pepper, grilled until soft,   ½ small clove garlic, chopped
   peeled and roughly chopped   salt and freshly ground black
1½ teaspoons sherry vinegar   pepper
2 tablespoons good olive oil

Put the pepper, vinegar, oil and garlic into a blender. Mix until smooth then add seasoning to taste.

Mayonnaise

Like vinaigrette, mayonnaise can be given innumerable different flavourings. These can come from the base ingredients – using a small proportion of nut oil or sesame oil; changing the vinegar, or using some orange, lime, tangerine, grapefruit or apple juice – or from the addition of flavours, such as grated citrus fruit rind or ginger, soy sauce, herbs, spices, or seasonings. The flavouring can either be added to the mayonnaise when it is being made, or a portion of already prepared mayonnaise can be flavoured to taste when it is needed.

1 small egg yolk or 1 small   1½–2 teaspoons white wine
   egg, at room temperature   vinegar, herb vinegar, or
1 scant teaspoon mustard   lemon juice
200–225 ml/7–8 fl oz oil, at   salt and freshly ground pepper
   room temperature

In a bowl, mix the egg yolk or whole egg with the mustard. Whisk in, drop by drop, 2 tablespoons of the oil, beating well after each addition. Then gradually whisk in the remaining oil, increasing the amount of each addition as the sauce thickens, and beating well after each addition.

If the sauce curdles or separates, try beating in 1 tablespoon very hot water, or gradually beating the curdled sauce into another egg yolk, which must also be at room temperature.

When all the oil is incorporated add vinegar or lemon juice and seasoning to taste.

Cover the surface closely with clingfilm and store the mayonnaise in a cool place; if this has to be the refrigerator, keep it as far away from the chilling unit as possible, such as in the door or salad drawer.

Keep for 2–3 days, or up to a week at most.

───────────── *Blender Mayonnaise* ─────────────

This has the dual advantage of being quick and almost infallible. Purists may say the results are not as good as the best conventionally made mayonnaise, but for most people, most of the time, the advantages outstrip any minor imperfections.

Use the same ingredients as above. Briefly blend the egg yolk or egg with the mustard then, with the motor running, gradually pour in the oil, adding it very slowly at first but more quickly as the mayonnaise thickens. Add about a third of the vinegar or lemon juice when about half the oil has been incorporated. When all the oil is mixed in, add the remaining vinegar or lemon juice and season to taste.

VARIATIONS

- Lemon Mayonnaise – add approximately 1½–2½ tablespoons lemon juice.
- Tarragon and Mustard Mayonnaise – put 1 small egg, 2 tablespoons lemon juice, 1 finely chopped spring onion or small shallot, and 1 teaspoon each Dijon and coarsegrain mustard into a blender then, with the motor running, slowly pour in 100ml/3½fl oz each vegetable oil and olive oil in a steady stream. Add 1 tablespoon finely chopped fresh tarragon or 1 teaspoon dried tarragon and seasoning to taste.

Aïoli

Although made in much the same way as mayonnaise, aïoli is a sauce in its own right, not simply garlic-flavoured mayonnaise. It should have the consistency of thick double cream, and can be made as mild or potent as you like by adjusting the amount of garlic and lemon juice used. If it does not thicken, or if it separates, pound or blend a small slice of crustless bread into the liquid.

4–10 cloves garlic, peeled	175ml/6fl oz olive oil
salt	approximately 1–1½
1 egg yolk	tablespoons lemon juice

Pound the garlic to a paste with a little salt then beat in the egg yolk. Continue to beat for about 1 minute until the mixture is thick and sticky.

Add the oil a drop at a time, beating with a wooden spoon or wire whisk all the time. When the sauce begins to thicken, which it should when about a third of the oil has been added, the oil can be added in a slow, thin trickle. Continue to beat all the time and make sure the oil is thoroughly incorporated. When about half the oil has been added, beat in about two-thirds of the lemon juice then continue to beat in the oil until the sauce is very thick. Add the remaining lemon juice to taste.

If using a blender or food processor, purée the garlic with a little salt, blend in the egg yolk and about two-thirds of the lemon juice for about 10 seconds then slowly pour in the oil to make a sauce with the consistency of thick double cream.

Almond Aïoli

3 cloves garlic
½ teaspoon salt
55g/2oz almonds, ground
4 tablespoons white wine
  vinegar or lemon juice

1 egg yolk
approximately 300ml/½ pint
  olive oil

Thoroughly crush the garlic with the salt in a pestle and mortar. Blend in the ground almonds, vinegar or lemon juice, and the egg yolk until smooth. Beat in the oil a drop at a time at first then more quickly, speeding up to a thin stream as the sauce begins to thicken. When ready, the sauce should have the consistency of soft butter.

Tapenade

Tapenade is a powerfully piquant southern French paste. I find it a wonderful fridge standby because it has so many uses – spread on crisp toast or good bread then topped with creamy scrambled eggs, or poached eggs, or cool slices of tomato, fromage blanc, or Brie in the peak of ripeness, or tossed with pasta (see page 91), or spread lightly over or served as a sauce with meats and poultry. It can be used neat or blended into mayonnaise, cream, fromage blanc or Greek yogurt, or beaten with butter.

There is no such thing as a definitive recipe for tapenade; use the one below as a starting point, and a base for experimenting with modifications and changes to proportions.

30g/1oz anchovy fillets,
  soaked in a little milk,
  drained and chopped
115g/4oz stoned black olives
1 tablespoon capers

½ teaspoon Dijon mustard
1 teaspoon lemon juice
approximately 2–3 teaspoons
  olive oil
freshly ground black pepper

Mix the anchovy fillets, olives, capers, mustard and lemon juice to a smooth paste using a pestle and mortar, blender or food processor. Gradually blend in the oil, season. Store in a screw-top jar in the refrigerator. Transfer to room temperature about 30 minutes before using.

VARIATION
● Add 1 tablespoon brandy.

— *Anchoïaide* —

Another French paste that I like to have in the fridge for giving an instant fillip to a wide range of foods (see Tapenade, page 240 for suggestions); I am constantly discovering new uses for it.

Spread on toasted French bread and accompanied by crudités or lightly dressed crisp salad leaves it makes a flavourful first course.

50g/1¾oz can anchovies in
  oil, drained
2 cloves garlic, chopped
1 tablespoon chopped fresh
  parsley

2–3 tablespoons extra-virgin
  olive oil
1 teaspoon red wine vinegar
freshly ground black pepper

Drain the anchovies, reserving the oil. Soak the fillets in warm milk or water for a few minutes then drain well on absorbent paper.

Either pound all the ingredients together in a pestle and

mortar, or simply mix everything together in a blender or food processor. Store in a screw-top jar in the refrigerator. Transfer to room temperature about 30 minutes before using.

VARIATIONS
- The addition of about 1 teaspoon tomato purée softens the flavour slightly without detracting from the character.
- Use some fresh basil and thyme instead of parsley, when available.
- Anchovy Butter – mix equal quantities of anchoïaide and unsalted butter with a few drops of lemon juice and freshly ground black pepper. Chill in the refrigerator until firm. Serve cold.

———— Black Olive and Walnut Paste ————

This paste keeps well in a covered jar in the refrigerator and can be used in many different ways – spread on toast, with eggs, or tossed with pasta or rice. Thin it down if necessary with a little stock or Greek yogurt, soured cream or fromage frais.

30g/1oz black olives, stoned and chopped
white part 1 medium spring onion, sliced
1 tablespoon coarsely chopped walnuts

1 scant tablespoon chopped fresh parsley
freshly ground black pepper
dash lemon juice

Put the olives, spring onion, walnuts and parsley into a blender and mix to a paste. Add black pepper and lemon juice to taste.

Aubergine Sauce

Even though the ingredients are few and simple this sauce has a wealth of complex flavours. It is very versatile, and tastes equally good hot or cold, so if it is not all used at once, the remainder can be served later in a completely different guise, and with different flavourings added if liked. Hot, it can be served over pasta (dilute the sauce with 2 teaspoons of the pasta cooking water), or with meats, poultry or fish; cold, it can be served as a dip for pitta bread or as a spread for bread or toast. Keep any that is not used immediately in a covered container in the refrigerator for a day or so.

It is also a good way of using a spare half an aubergine.

1 small aubergine
1 clove garlic, crushed
  (optional)
approximately 2 tablespoons
  extra-virgin olive oil

lemon juice (optional)
salt and freshly ground black
  pepper

Grill the aubergine then remove the skin. Gently squeeze the flesh to expel the juices. Blend the flesh in a blender or food processor with the garlic, if using, while slowly pouring in the oil. Add a little lemon juice, if liked, salt and plenty of pepper.

VARIATIONS

- Add a small pinch of toasted cumin seeds to the aubergine flesh before puréeing.
- Aubergine and Tahina Sauce – omit the oil, and add 1–2 tablespoons tahina and about 2 teaspoons lemon juice to the aubergine purée; cumin seeds can also be added.
- Flavour the purée with a pinch of paprika pepper.
- For a light sauce that is low in calories, omit the oil and add 1–2 tablespoons fromage blanc and either cumin seeds or paprika.

——————————— *Flavoured Butters* ———————————

These take only minutes to make but are useful not only for spreading on bread and toast but also for tossing with pasta and rice, serving with meat, poultry and fish, dotting on to cooked vegetables, and beating into vegetable purées.

Simply beat the flavouring into softened unsalted butter, adding a little lemon juice if necessary to lift the flavour. Store in a covered pot or jar, or wrapped in clingfilm or polythene, in the refrigerator or a cool place.

To 175g/6oz softened unsalted butter, add:

Anchovy – approximately 6–8 anchovy fillets that have been soaked in a little milk, then drained, plus a squeeze of lemon juice and some freshly ground black pepper.
Garlic – 3 cloves finely crushed garlic.
Green peppercorn – 1 tablespoon chopped green peppercorns.
Herb – approximately 3 tablespoons finely chopped fresh herbs and 1 tablespoon lemon juice.
Horseradish – 1 tablespoon horseradish relish.
Lemon – 2 tablespoons lemon juice and 1 tablespoon lemon rind.
Lime – 2 tablespoons each lime juice and rind.
Mustard – 2 tablespoons mustard.
Nut – 55g/2oz finely chopped nuts.
Orange – 1½ tablespoons each orange rind and juice.

Taste the butter after adding the flavouring and adjust the balance, if necessary, with more butter, flavouring or lemon juice.

Chicken Stock

Makes about 500ml/18fl oz.

500g/1lb chicken carcasses
veal knuckle bone, chopped
  (optional)
1 small onion, stuck with a
  clove
1 small carrot, sliced

1 small stick celery, chopped
white part 1 leek, sliced
bouquet garni of 1 small bay
  leaf, 2 parsley stalks, small
  sprig thyme and sprig
  chervil

Put the chicken carcasses and veal bone, if using, into a saucepan, add about 1 litre/1¾ pints water, and bring to the boil. Remove the scum from the surface, add the vegetables and bouquet garni, return to the boil then simmer for about 2–3 hours to reduce by half, removing the scum from the surface frequently. Pass the stock through a sieve lined with muslin or cheesecloth, leave to cool then remove the fat from the surface.

Fish Stock

Makes about 550ml/1 pint.

unsalted butter
1 shallot, quartered
white part 1 small leek,
  chopped
30g/1oz button mushrooms,
  chopped
500g/1lb fish bones, heads and

trimmings, soaked in cold
  water, rinsed
5 tablespoons medium-bodied
  dry white wine
bouquet garni of 1 small bay
  leaf, 2 small parsley stalks
  and 1 small sprig fennel

Melt a small knob of butter in a pan, add the vegetables, cover and cook over a moderate heat, shaking the pan occasionally, for

4–5 minutes. Add the fish bones, heads and trimmings and cook, stirring, for a further 2–3 minutes. Stir in the wine, boil until reduced by half then add the bouquet garni followed by 875ml/ 1½ pints water. Bring to the boil then simmer for about 25 minutes, removing the scum from the surface frequently. Pass the stock through a sieve lined with muslin or cheesecloth, leave to cool then remove the fat from the surface.

—————— *Vegetable Stock* ——————

Makes about 500ml/18fl oz.

unsalted butter
1 shallot, finely chopped
white part 1 small leek, finely chopped
½ carrot, finely chopped
½ teaspoon fennel seeds

1 tomato, chopped
bouquet garni of 1 parsley stalk, 1 small bay leaf, small sprig chervil, and small sprig thyme
½ teaspoon white peppercorns

Melt a small knob of butter, add the shallot and leek, cover and cook over a low heat, shaking the pan occasionally, until the shallot has softened. Stir in the remaining ingredients and 600ml/ 1 pint 2fl oz cold water, bring to the boil, skim the scum from the surface then simmer for about 20 minutes, removing the scum from the surface frequently. Pass the stock through a sieve lined with muslin or cheesecloth, leave to cool then remove the fat from the surface.

INDEX